Stay bounc_

♡ Ka Srl___

"When you're falling,
dive."

–JOSEPH CAMPBELL

BY KAREN SALMANSOHN

THE
BOUNCE
BACK
BOOK

how to **thrive** in the face of adversity,
setbacks, and losses

WORKMAN PUBLISHING • NEW YORK

Library of Congress Cataloging-in-Publication Data:
Salmansohn, Karen.
The bounce back book : how to thrive in the face of adversity, setbacks and losses /
by Karen Salmansohn.
ISBN=13: 978-0-7611-4627-8 (alk. paper)
1. Resilience (Personality trait) I. Title.
BF698.35.R47S35 2007
650.1 dc22   2007042773

Workman books are available at special discounts when purchased in bulk for premiums and sales promotions as well as for fund-raising or educational use. Special editions or book excerpts also can be created to specification. For details, contact the Special Sales Director at the address below.

Design by **Grip Design**
Art direction: **Kelly Kaminski, Kevin McConkey**
Cover and interior design: **Nikki Lo Bue**
Design assistance: **Camay Ho**

Book packager: **Karen Salmansohn**

"Autobiography in Five Short Chapters." Copyright 1993, by Portia Nelson from the book *There's a Hole in My Sidewalk,* Beyond Words Publishing, Hillsboro, OR.

"The Guest House" by Rumi, translated by Coleman Barks, reprinted with permission of Coleman Barks.

Workman Publishing Company, Inc.
225 Varick Street
New York, NY 10014-4381
www.workman.com

Printed in China

First printing March 2008
10 9 8 7 6 5 4 3 2 1

The **Vortex,** I call it.

Everyone has one in their life (at least one)—a time when you are tested in seemingly insurmountable ways and things continue to go wrong, and you spiral uncontrollably downward.

Maybe your Vortex was when you were **13** and a parent suddenly died.

Or **24** and you found out your sister had breast cancer and you got fired, both in the same month.

Or **29** and discovering you could not have a child.

Or **42** and going through a divorce.

Or **51** and happily retiring, only to discover playing golf all day was a formula for depression.

My Vortex lasted about a year, during which time so many bad things happened, I kept waiting for a *Candid Camera* crew to appear from behind the planter in my living room. First, the real estate broker, real estate lawyer, and moving company I hired found sneaky ways to rip me off. Next, a longtime business buddy hired me to package new groovy chocolate bars, then never paid me.

But those were nothing compared to the lowest point in my Vortex: a sexual assault—which came out of nowhere—by someone I knew as an acquaintance. As soon as I managed to get free and far away from my assaulter, I called my close friend Eric Gertler, an ex-boyfriend and ex-lawyer. I figured because he knew both the law and me intimately, he'd be a wise adviser. We met at our regular café. I was in tears.

"How could someone be so…so…so evil?" I asked.
"People aren't evil. They're weak," said Eric.
Weak? This word somehow calmed me.

Later when I tried to understand why I preferred the word "weak" to the word "evil," I realized that "weakness" meant there was at least hope for change in someone who'd done something evil—and most importantly, hope for me to find a way out of my Vortex by choosing not to be weak myself.

That's when it hit me. In life, you always have a choice. Be **weak** or be **strong**.

Whichever of these paths you choose will determine your ability to bounce back from life's myriad setbacks, crises, or traumas. If you want to survive life's many challenges, you must put in the conscious effort and discipline to be a strong person. It's essential you create a fiery will from within—harness that power of decisiveness—and choose to be your strongest self.

Initially I was totally traumatized by my sexual assault. I started experiencing anxiety around people. If I'd be writing in a café and a stranger chatted me up, my left eye would twitch. And no, it wasn't the caffeine. (Trust me. I'm a pro at espresso. And I'm a pro at casual conversation with strangers.)

Basically, after the assault my automatic tendency was to keep all people at a distance. I had trouble trusting anyone. Even people I'd known for years. After all, I'd witnessed how people could change in a moment. And so I pretty much became paranoid about everyone I came into contact with. Especially men.

Then I gained weight—12 pounds—which is a ton on my 5-foot-3 frame. Maybe subconsciously I figured there was safety in creating a big wad of fat between me and men's sexual urges. It was easy to gain weight. I had all this chocolate around my apartment from the nonpaying chocolate business buddy. He was a bad businessman, but he made some damn good chocolate!

Soon enough, this upward weight gain created a further downward emotional spiral. I began feeling bummed about my bigger bum, which further increased my yearning to stay inside away from people and close to my chocolate bars.

I was a self-help author! Why couldn't I help myself get through this? Sometimes, when I saw the growing discrepancy between who I was and how I was behaving, I'd mutter to myself in a kind of mock-voiceover: "Behind the scenes of the self-help book author…" as I unwrapped another chocolate bar.

Honestly, I was surprised I'd chosen this weaker path of chocolate and withdrawal into solitude.

I've always thought of myself as a very strong person, as have those who know me well. My friend David once introduced me at a party as "This is Karen. She's a 'doer.'" Most of my friends see me as disciplined and spirited. In my heart I believed this "disciplined and spirited me" was the real me. Yet if I wasn't being "disciplined and spirited" during a crisis, was I truly this me or somebody else entirely? I pondered this more and eventually realized:

Who you *truly* are as a person is best revealed by who you are during times of conflict and crisis.

It's easy to be your strongest, highest self when things are rolling along smoothly. But how you handle life's setbacks and traumas reveals your authentic character. If you can be strong during challenging times, then…well, you truly ARE a disciplined and spirited person. And this identity makes you not only a very cool person but a very happy person.

Just as it takes willpower to choose to stay on a healthy diet during times of great temptation, it also takes willpower to choose to remain a positive and happy human being during times of crisis. Basically, to live a happy life—with all of life's multiple challenges—takes effort and work. Happiness is not for namby-pambies! For this reason, you need to develop a long-term vision for what you uniquely value—what you know makes you the happiest—so you can stay focused on these values, no matter what your trials and tribulations.

I know what I value: I need to feel loving, loved, creatively charged, healthy, sexy, self-confident, and as if I am continuously growing. (Note: not in thighs but in mind and spirit!) I also know: Life is constantly testing our ability to feel those things.

Actually, if there were a single instructional goal for living your best life it might be "Keep your eye on the prize of happiness, even when caught in the eye of the storm—or Vortex."

Guess what else? Lucky unlucky us: Often the greatest happiness in life comes from going through a crisis—and growing into a stronger, better person. In fact, Aristotle, one of my favorite philosophers, wrote in great detail about how true happiness does not come from experiencing pleasures of the body and ego but from having experiences that stimulate your core self—your "soul"—challenging and inspiring you to grow into your highest potential as a person.

You know how sharks need to keep on moving to stay alive? We humans need to consciously keep on moving forward emotionally if we want to keep our spirits alive—or else our spirits will fizzle and fade. Basically, you're either growing into a bigger, better person or shrinking into a lowly, bitter person. And by "growing," I don't mean simply reading lots of self-help books, doing yoga, eating granola bars, and having highfalutin', ego-tootin' intellectual conversations.

There's an old expression: "There are those who know where it is, they just don't know WHAT it is." It doesn't matter how many books you read or meditation classes you take if you're only going through the motions without experiencing true inner growth.

So WHAT *is* "growing"? Putting in the emotional effort to improve who you are as a person—facing your core pain—and working to stretch yourself to become your strongest, wisest, highest-level self. Yes, I believe the greatest reward out there is actually not OUT there at all. It's an INSIDE job! The greatest reward is knowing that you are refusing to settle for being anything less than you can be. And there's nothing more fulfilling and thrilling than discovering yourself to be a stronger person than you ever dreamed yourself capable of being.

My Vortex made me who I am today, and the good news is, I actually like myself more because of it. My Vortex challenged me to make that choice:

1. Be weak.   2. Be strong.

And when push came to shove, I chose "be strong," baby!

In the movie *Wag the Dog,* every time Dustin Hoffman's character faced a new challenge in his TV production, he kept repeating, "This is nothing! This is NOTHING!" I relate. After going through my Vortex, I now feel better prepared to deal with future challenges that lie ahead. And you know what? Unlucky things will continue to happen to me. And not just to me, to everyone. We might not like it, but unlucky events are as much a "given" on this earth as gravity.

You might as well accept the reality now: Your life will continue to have ebbs and flows. There's no such thing as endless flow. Unfortunately, life can sometimes feel like ebb, ebb, ebb, brief-flash-of-flow, more ebb, ebb. And so it's essential to develop the right coping tools for dealing with life's all too plentiful challenges.

There's an old Buddhist expression that goes something like: "A man can't cover up all the infinite stone-covered, jagged paths of this world with a layer of soft, cushy leather. But a man can wear soft, cushy leather sandals on the soles of his feet to protect himself on the journey." Ditto for unlucky events. You can't rid them from this planet. But you can develop the coping tools, techniques, and philosophies to protect yourself—and give yourself the wherewithal to keep moving forward. That's where this book comes in. My goal in writing *The Bounce Back Book* was to share with you all the tools and lessons I learned during my return from my Vortex.

In the pages ahead you will find 75 Tips grounded in happiness research, medical studies, positive psychology, Eastern meditation, even Greek philosophy; in each one I've distilled the wisdom of an expert to a short, easily-digestible, potentially life-changing tip on how to bounce back from adversity—along with the research that makes it so compelling. I've also included in some of the "Bounce Back Assignments" actual exercises and techniques from therapists to help you reframe your challenges so you will be able to think differently about them—and thereby be able to *feel* differently about them.

I recognize that one book cannot be all things to all people at the same time. Some of you reading this book might be recovering from a deep personal tragedy while others may be going through a life setback that challenges you in different ways. As a result, some Tips in this book will be more appropriate and helpful than others depending on the nature of your trauma and where you are in the process of recovery. I'm hoping that the majority of the Tips will be immediately inspiring and useful. But if you find some of the suggestions "too light" for the heavy burden you're dealing with right now, feel free to skip past them and consider returning to them when you're further along in your recovery.

And, as usual in my serious self-help books, I use humor because I believe humor is a terrific "enlightening device"—immediately lightening your mood—getting you outside of yourself, so you can experience that needed enlightenment!

Finally, everything I'm preaching in this book, I practiced. It works.

Wishing you strength in abundance,

Karen

KAREN SALMANSOHN

Forward

If you're expecting this to be a typical foreword to a book, it's not. It's far better. It's your first empowering Bounce Back Tip…

tip#1: Be a forward thinker.

BOUNCE BACK ASSIGNMENT

Whenever you're tempted to dwell in the past, repeat this single word: **forward.** Brainstorm one positive thought and action to use to keep you moving **forward.** When you're tempted to indulge in a negative, regressive behavior, swap it for one that will **move you forward.**

tip#

What you are going
through now is **normal.**

tip# **3**

There is no such thing as **normal.**

You are not alone. You are not being singled out by the fates to suffer.

Everyone has times of intense difficulties. These difficulties can be illness, divorce, job loss, miscarriage, ego-shattering failure, heartbreak, assault, physical trauma, betrayal, economic hardship, and then some…

Perhaps you recognize yourself a few times in these categories. And that's okay. Even normal. You've been sideswiped. Maybe even frontswiped.

Yes, life comes with a vast array of surprises.

Their aftereffects are equally varied.

Emotional: depression, anxiety, fear, stress, anger, guilt, grief, shame, shaken self-esteem, feeling lost, overwhelmed.

Cognitive: poor concentration, shortened attention span, memory problems, difficulty making decisions, recurring thoughts, nightmares, flashbacks.

Physical: muscle tremors, chest pain, difficulty breathing, headaches, high blood pressure.

Behavioral: withdrawal, increased alcohol consumption, sleep disturbances, changes in eating, disruption of work habits, lack of sexual interest.

Recognize: All of these aftereffects are normal reactions.

Recognize: Just as physical wounds heal at different rates in different people, so do emotional wounds. Everyone has different needs and speeds.

* * * * * * * * * * * * * * * * *

Bounce Back Assignment:

Don't put added pressure on yourself to hurry back to normal. There is no such thing as normal. What's important is that you're **nurturing your wounds appropriately,** instead of nudging them to heal so rapidly that you bruise yourself further in the process.

tip# **4**

Feeling means
you're dealing
means you're
healing.

I was experiencing many of the same emotions after my sexual assault that Elisabeth Kübler-Ross describes in her five stages of accepting the death of a loved one. The only difference is that, with death, you at least get the perk of being brought some yummy casseroles.

Kübler-Ross outlined the five stages of grief as follows:

STAGE #1: DENIAL AND ISOLATION:
"This is not happening to me."

STAGE #2: ANGER:
"How dare this happen to me."

STAGE #3: BARGAINING:
"Just let me get X and I won't care about Y," or "If this doesn't happen, I promise to…"

STAGE #4: DEPRESSION:
"I can't bear to face going through this."

STAGE #5: ACCEPTANCE:
"I'm ready; I don't want to struggle anymore."

In her memoir *The Year of Magical Thinking,* Joan Didion describes how after the sudden death of her husband at the dinner table, she found herself focused on who she needed to call, what she needed to do, what the hospital needed from her (getting copies of medical summaries, patiently standing in line to fill out forms, etc.). But what appeared to those around her to be a preternatural calm ("She's a pretty cool customer!" Didion overheard a hospital social worker say) was in fact a state of total numbness.

Unable to face the reality of her husband's death, Didion found herself engaging in what she calls "magical thinking," a conjuring of a world in which her husband might reappear. She avoids reading John's obituary, believing it a form of betrayal; she tells herself she must keep John's shoes because he would need them when he "comes back"; she wonders if perhaps things would have turned out differently had they been dining in California that night rather than New York.

Eventually, however, Didion discovers what most of us discover: When it comes to emotional pain, you can run…but you can't hide.

If you've been through a personal tragedy, chances are that you too don't want to accept it and let in all the painful emotions—at least for a while.

Psychologist Sharon Wolf believes there is a "core pain" you must be ready to feel during really bad times to fully recover: "If you want to heal rightly from a crisis, be ready to tolerate more pain than you thought you could ever feel," warns Wolf.

Thankfully, Wolf promises *if you learn to sit with, feel, and tolerate this core pain, it will get smaller and smaller, until it ultimately disappears.*

Or as I learned from my own travels through these stages: "Feeling means you're dealing means you're healing." After numbing myself to the pain and living in denial and isolation, when my core pain finally did arrive, it was in a full-blown stage 4 depression—in the form of a crying jag that lasted for a full 2 weeks.

During this time, I'd be walking around, feeling just fine, thank you, la-de-da de-da. Then suddenly, like a tidal wave—fawhomp—whoooosh!!—the floodgates would open. The unbearable sadness I'd been evading finally had caught up with me and grabbed me by the throat so I couldn't breathe.

And though I dreaded those tears and the total loss of control, I found out later this was actually a good and necessary thing.

If you're going through a challenging time, it's essential you recognize that it's your choice to:

1. Sit with the pain now **or**

2. Avoid the pain now and feel even greater pain later, thereby delaying the healing.

In the wonderful book *The Buddha and the Terrorist,* Satish Kumar writes, "Sister, pain is part of life. By accepting it, its intensity is reduced. Do not resist it. Resistance to pain brings tension and anxiety, anxiety leads to fear. Fear of pain is worse than pain itself. This pain will pass."

✳ ✳ ✳ ✳ ✳ ✳ ✳ ✳ ✳ ✳ ✳ ✳ ✳ ✳

BOUNCE BACK ASSIGNMENT:

If you are avoiding your pain and grief as I tried to do, remind yourself:

1. **Fear of pain is often worse than the pain itself.** When the pain starts to seep through to your consciousness, let it come. Don't fight those tears. If possible, give yourself specific times to grieve. (By the way, as an unexpected perk, crying is better than getting a facial in removing toxins for clear, glowing skin.)

2. **Because feeling your core pain is scary, you might be tempted to seek comfort** by numbing yourself—with alcohol, sleeping pills, or other addictive substances. Be strong. Resist and persist in allowing your true pain to surface.

3. **You are an unfinished self in progress.** Like so many of life's challenges, experiencing and overcoming pain can reveal emotional depths and perspectives you didn't know you were capable of.

4. **Keep a journal.** Track your healing process through the five stages (you may skip some stages and also regress or cycle back), but a journal will show you that **progress is being made.** And remember, after you pass through stage 4, that final stage of Acceptance is right around the corner! Whew!

tip#**5**

Turn over a **new belief.**

"Experience is not what happens to a man; it is what a man does with what happens to him."
—ALDOUS HUXLEY

"We are what we think. All that we are arises with our thoughts. With our thoughts, we create our world." —BUDDHA

"Drugs are not always necessary, [but] belief in recovery always is." —NORMAN COUSINS

"Things do not change, we change."
—HENRY DAVID THOREAU

"Man's mind stretched to a new idea never goes back to its original dimensions."
—OLIVER WENDELL HOLMES JR.

"The best is yet to come."
—FRANK SINATRA

BOUNCE BACK ASSIGNMENT:
Let better beliefs grow strong.

tip#

The part is
not greater than
the whole.

BOUNCE BACK ASSIGNMENT:

Yo! Remember. This bad time you are going through right now is merely **IN** your life. It is not your **WHOLE** life. So be sure to keep this slice of your life in perspective—and not let it overwhelm.

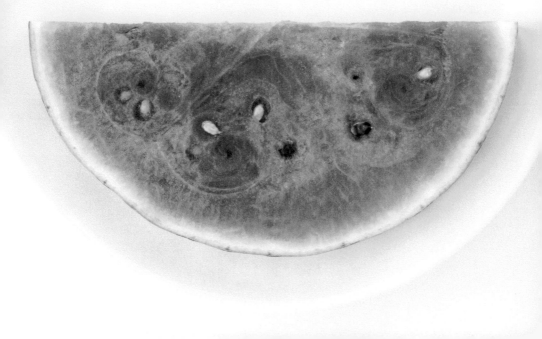

tip#

Think like a lion.

A star lion tamer with Barnum & Bailey Circus, Graham Thomas Chipperfield, got bitten by Sheba, one of his 500-pound lionesses.

Before the mauled tamer got back into the cage, he made very sure to see what happened from Sheba's point of view. He recognized how lions tend to think of the trainer as another lion. And so when he bounded into the cage to break up a fight between Sheba and another lion, Sheba merely figured Chipperfield wanted to join in the fight too.

Did Chipperfield sit around blaming Sheba for her inaccurate thinking? No. Instead he took the time to see the biting from Sheba's perspective, so he'd make sure this bad event would not happen again.

Robert Staub, a psychologist who counsels people who have been through failure, would agree with the Chipperfield philosophy. He says that the main cause of career and relationship failure is "not being able to adopt the viewpoint of others."

For this reason, many therapists—beginning with Freud—have clients role-play a situation from the offending party's perspective. The hope is that by understanding why someone might have emotionally taken a bite out of them, the patient can avoid being bitten again!

✳ ✳ ✳ ✳ ✳ ✳ ✳ ✳ ✳ ✳ ✳ ✳ ✳ ✳ ✳

Bounce Back Assignment:

Take the time today to understand your contribution to any bad event you've just been through.

Never, ever put yourself back into the same environment—**a marriage, a job, a friendship**—until you've fully understood things from "the lion's point of view."

tip# 8

A Rolling Stones fan gathers **less loss.**

BOUNCE BACK ASSIGNMENT:

When feeling down, put on a little Rolling Stones and dance it on up. Contemplate as you gyrate how although you might not be getting everything you want in your life, maybe you are getting what you need!

tip#

It's not only the event itself,
but the way we explain
the event to ourselves
that causes depression.

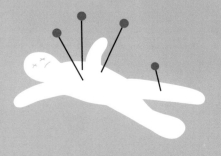

Dr. Martin Seligman, director of the University of Pennsylvania's Positive Psychology Center, says bouncing back up from bad times depends on "the stories" you tell yourself.

These stories, or "self-talk," can either enable you to persist in the face of failure or disable you and make you downright miserable. "Pessimists, who generally don't bounce back easily from bad times, see setbacks as permanent, pervasive, and personal," says Seligman.

Optimistic people, in contrast, tell themselves that setbacks are temporary, confined to that one situation, and are usually about the other person, not a character defect in themselves. They tend to assume that bad events are an exception, and good things will continue to happen.

But even the gloomiest of pessimists can learn to be more optimistic, Seligman argues in his book, *Learned Optimism.* We are all capable of changing the way we think about an event, which will change our feelings about it *and* the consequences it has on our life.

You can't change your past, but you *can* control its effects on your future.

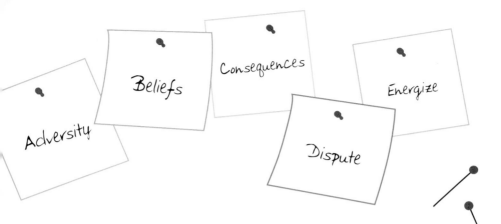

Dr. Seligman and his colleague Dr. Karen Reivich have created a specific process for bouncing back, one that's literally as easy as **A B C D E**:

Here's how it works: When we encounter **Adversity**, we react by thinking about it and our thoughts congeal into **Beliefs**. These beliefs have **Consequences**: They determine how we feel and how we act and they can spell the difference between dejection and constructive action. The first step is to see the connection between **A**, **B**, and **C** and how it operates in your own life…then do something about it. **D**ispute the negative beliefs, and you'll find that your **E**nergy will change. Here's how:

In a journal, write down those five letters and your answers to the following questions:

1. Start by spelling out the nature of your **ADVERSITY**. Describe the who, what, when, and where of the situation as objectively as possible.

2. What **BELIEFS** has your Adversity triggered? What type of person does it make you feel like? What kind of world does it make you feel you live in? To identify your **BELIEFS**, slow down and listen to your self-talk, specifically for comments that sound "permanent, pervasive, and personal," for example, "I'll never get a job" (permanent). "This always happens" (pervasive). "I'm an idiot" (personal). Our beliefs are so habitual, we don't even realize we have them unless we stop and focus on them. It takes practice to identify your self-defeating Beliefs. *Listen to yourself. Take some notes on the chatter in your brain.*

3. Describe the **CONSEQUENCES** of your Beliefs. How are you feeling? How are you behaving? Become aware of how your wrongly held beliefs might be triggering negative behaviors. Is there anything you've stopped doing? Any new habits you've picked up? For example: Pigging out. Drinking. Yelling at loved ones. Not trying new opportunities. In other words, how has your Adversity changed you?

4. DISPUTE what you've written so far with specific evidence that points out the flaws in your Beliefs. Question the reality and accuracy of your interpretation. For example, *I'll never get a job.* (Is that true? Says who? Have there been times when you thought you'd never find work and did?) *This always happens.* (Can you think of an exception?) *I'm an idiot.* (Compared to? What is your definition of idiot, anyway? Have there been times when you've shown practical or academic smarts?) Come up with an alternative (and more accurate) way of looking at what happened. For example: "Maybe this person broke up with me not because I'm fat, but because he has fear of commitment. After all, he is 50 and never married!"

5. ENERGIZE. When you have been effective in disputing false beliefs, you often feel a surge of energy, a sense of renewed hope. Write how your answers to #4 changed your mood.

❅ ❅ ❅ ❅ ❅ ❅ ❅ ❅ ❅ ❅ ❅ ❅ ❅ ❅ ❅ ❅

Bounce Back Assignment:

Stop the "negative loop" of self-defeating self-stories. Swap feeling like you're wearing a **"KICK ME"** sign to feeling like you're wearing a **"KICK ASS"** sign!

tip#  10

Happiness is a choice,
not just a matter of
genes or good luck.

According to researchers at The Happiness Project in the U.K., our genetic inheritance towards optimism (happiness) or pessimism is only about 50%. So with the other 50% you're able to make new choices.

Translation: This is good news! It means you control that other 50% of your reaction to life's difficulties and can do things to change your happiness level.

Easier said than done, right? Well, positive psychologist Dr. Jonathan Haidt has devised a very useful formula for how to be happier:

$$H = S + C + V$$

H = level of happiness   **C** = current conditions

S = set point for happiness   **V** = voluntary activities

In other words, your happiness level is a potent mix of how naturally happy you are (that 50% figure) combined with whatever's going on in your life right now that affects your happiness, plus those voluntary activities you choose to fill your life with. (There's that word **choose** again!)

✳ ✳ ✳ ✳ ✳ ✳ ✳ ✳ ✳ ✳ ✳ ✳ ✳ ✳ ✳

Bounce Back Assignment:

If your happiness level isn't registering high enough because current conditions are dragging you down, forget about what you can't control and focus on those **V's.** Those **V**oluntary activities.

Decide to add more **"ING"** to your life. By **"ING"** I mean runn-**ING**, hik-**ING**, cook-**ING**, salsa danc-**ING**, cycl-**ING**, paint-**ING**—do-**ING** things that make you happy. Whatever they are, make sure they make you feel **V**ital, **V**ibrant, **V**a **V**a **V**oom, **V**ictorious!

tip# **11**

If you ask depressing
questions, you will 100%
get depressing **answers.**

Are you asking yourself questions that further weigh you down?

Why didn't I...?   **What if...?**   **Why me?**

Would you accept some of the mean and nasty questions you ask yourself if they came from an outside source?

If not, then stop and swap them immediately for these questions that bounce you upward:

WHAT CAN I DO to move forward?

HOW CAN I GROW from this challenge?

WHAT'S WITHIN MY CONTROL to change?

✻ ✻ ✻ ✻ ✻ ✻ ✻ ✻ ✻ ✻ ✻ ✻ ✻ ✻ ✻ ✻ ✻

Bounce Back Assignment:

Next time a question pops into your head, ask yourself, **"Is this a non-bounceable question?"** If it is, drop it. And watch out for your toes!

tip# **12**

Don't ride a
roller coaster
of feelings.

You're probably dealing with some pretty powerful emotions right now, but how are you *feeling*?

Yup, it turns out there's a difference between emotions and feelings.

Feelings are your learned habitual responses inputted into your brain after a defining personal experience. For example, you might "feel" a fear of bikes because you fell off one at age 3.

Emotions, in contrast, are humans' primal urges. Grief, for example, is a universal emotional response to death.

But how you feel when you are grieving depends on your culture and your personal history—in other words, your learned habitual responses.

You may not be able to do much about your personal history or your culture, but it's helpful to be aware that your past might be affecting your present *feelings* during tough times, triggering a roller-coaster ride of feelings you thought you left behind a long time ago.

For Example: The death of someone in your present can often retrigger the pain you felt over a death in your past—or even a parent's divorce, which can *feel* a lot like a death.

In other words, some of these "feelings" you're dealing with right now actually stem from your past, not your current situation.

It's important in times of trauma to be able to pick through the prickly pile of feelings and emotions and separate your direct emotional response to your current situation from your bad "feeling habits."

Understandably, during a Vortex mode, it's normal to have some recurring negative thoughts, nightmares, and scary flashbacks. BUT if you feel yourself riding a roller coaster of highs and plummeting lows that you don't see coming, take the time to analyze where your negative feelings are coming from.

 WARNING: If you find that your roller-coaster ride is going on way longer than you're comfortable with and it's way bumpier than you'd like, please consider getting professional help. Some habits are awfully hard to break, and sometimes we need a helping hand to get to the heart of a problem we may be too close to see.

✳ ✳ ✳ ✳ ✳ ✳ ✳ ✳ ✳ ✳ ✳ ✳ ✳ ✳ ✳

BOUNCE BACK ASSIGNMENT:

ASK YOURSELF:

- What current feelings are **familiar?**

- Can I think of any feelings from the **past** that this present crisis might be retriggering?

- Can I **remember** how I worked through it at the time?

Even just understanding the source is a way to lessen its impact. Separate out which feelings are your bad "feeling habits," and don't let them get in the way of dealing with your present emotional trauma.

ASK YOURSELF:

- What are my triggers for **joy?**
  Surround yourself with them!

ADMIT ONE

061807

061807

tip# 13
cloud

watch

Bounce Back Assignment:

Imagine your troubles floating away with the clouds.

tip# **14**

Reframe
your life.

Be a student, not a victim. Find the meaning in the bad and learn lessons from life. Viktor Frankl, a psychologist who survived three years in a concentration camp, wrote an inspiring book about the benefits of student-not-victim mentality called *Man's Search for Meaning.* Frankl purports that those who survived concentration camps were not necessarily more physically robust. Survivors chose to find meaning in their suffering, which kept them alive and thriving.

In other words, they had a student, not victim, mentality. Frankl practiced what he preached. He believed he was meant to survive the Holocaust so he could write about the search for meaning and help others survive terrible times.

✳ ✳ ✳ ✳ ✳ ✳ ✳ ✳ ✳ ✳ ✳ ✳ ✳ ✳ ✳ ✳ ✳

Bounce Back Assignment:

When feeling down, recite this Frankl quote:

"It isn't the past which holds us back, it's the future; and how we undermine it, today."

tip# **15**

Find Your Bounceable People.

According to Aristotle, we humans are biologically social animals and our "first nature" is to be around people. However, I personally discovered that after my trauma, being around people felt much more like my 2,841st nature. It's common to want to hide away. But studies show it's far more healthful to seek support.

Dr. Dina Carbonell of Simmons College studied the secrets of people who successfully bounced back from hard times. She tracked 400 people from ages 5 to 30 for 25 years, studying the main characteristics of those who did best in difficult circumstances. She found that: "Resilient people identify those who are available, trustworthy, and helpful. Then they go toward this light."

But how do you know which people are good to be around when you're in crisis mode? Sometimes those friends we thought we could count on aren't there for us now. Make a list of 10 people you consider friends. Now ask yourself: Who is 100% rooting for you to live your happiest life—and not competing or jealous? Who do you always feel happier after visiting, not more depressed? These are your bounceable people: your support hive.

❋ ❋ ❋ ❋ ❋ ❋ ❋ ❋ ❋ ❋ ❋ ❋ ❋ ❋ ❋ ❋

Bounce Back Assignment:

Make sure you are playing the right amount of **hide-and-seek.** Spend a few hours a week with your bounceable people via e-mail or on the phone. Better yet, spend in-person time with them.

REMEMBER: One of the indirectly good things about going through bad times is that it can bring you closer to others because in your openness and vulnerability, you often bond in a deeper, more emotionally meaningful way.

Write a complaint letter.
Then answer it.

* * * * * * * * * * * * *

BOUNCE BACK ASSIGNMENT:

Scribble out every fleeting thought of worry, anger, fear, shame, self-pity. Ask for **comfort, insight, strength, courage.** When you're done writing, reread your letter and then reply to yourself. Pretend you are the offending individual or a higher power from whom you are seeking relief and solace.

What might they say to you to make you feel better? **Write it or say it to yourself NOW.**

tip# **17**

The only true observer of your world and your issues is **you.**

During bad times, if you feel embarrassed by what others are thinking about you, fear not. Most people aren't thinking about all the things wrong in your world. They're too caught up with all the things wrong in their own worlds.

BOUNCE BACK ASSIGNMENT:

Don't focus on what others are thinking. Trust your instincts. Do only what your gut tells you is right for you.

Q: If we didn't complain,
what would we
have to talk about?

A: Plenty.

✳ ✳ ✳ ✳ ✳ ✳ ✳ ✳ ✳ ✳ ✳ ✳ ✳ ✳

BOUNCE BACK ASSIGNMENT:

You've been through tough times. It's normal to want to vent. Here's the deal on complaining.

1. You're allowed to air all complaints three times—to get them out of your system. But once a complaint hits the air that third time, you must **let it turn into vapor.**

2. If you have to bring up the same complaint a fourth time, it should be:
a. in an effort to see a new insight
b. in the hope of fixing a problem
c. with the goal of improving your long-term life plan

3. Oh—and you're also allowed to complain a fourth time if it's in a really, really funny way. In fact, joking about your ordeal can be highly cathartic for you—and a lot more fun for your listener.

tip# **19**

Walk yourself out of
that **bad mood.**

𝒜 well-known research study at Duke University showed that going for a brisk 30-minute walk three times a week is as effective as taking antidepressants to improve your mood. And the researchers found that those who exercised had more long-lasting benefits than those who took antidepressants.

Why? Exercise increases the release of endorphins and the mood-enhancing neurotransmitter serotonin in the brain, the same chemicals that antidepressants manipulate to make you feel better.

Researchers also discovered that during exercise there is an increase in the brain's emission of alpha waves that are associated with a relaxed, meditation-like state. This feeling appears about 20 minutes into a 30-minute exercise session.

✳ ✳ ✳ ✳ ✳ ✳ ✳ ✳ ✳ ✳ ✳ ✳ ✳ ✳ ✳ ✳

Bounce Back Assignment:

Take some steps toward improving your mood today.
Step outside for a walk or a run.

tip# 20

If you can drive
yourself crazy...
you can drive
yourself happy.

* * * * * * * * * * * * * * *

BOUNCE BACK ASSIGNMENT:

Use the same techniques you currently use to make yourself feel bitter to aid and abet you in feeling better.

1. Instead of being paranoid, be **"pro-noid."** Start believing people are conspiring in your favor.

2. Instead of surrounding yourself with nutsy people, surround yourself with **positive people.**

tip# 21

When life throws you curveballs, hit them out of the park.

If you've been fired…consider starting your own company.

If you've had a bad breakup…consider moving to another city or country.

If you've been faced with an illness…consider training to run a marathon and becoming your healthiest self ever.

✳ ✳ ✳ ✳ ✳ ✳ ✳ ✳ ✳ ✳ ✳ ✳ ✳ ✳ ✳ ✳

Bounce Back Assignment:

Change is good, if you **INSIST** on making change be good. Don't fight it. **Embrace it.** Go with the flow of your change by considering flowing in a whole new direction. Brainstorm crazy new ideas that are now newly possible! Keep in mind Joseph Campbell's words: **"If you are falling, dive!"**

tip# 22

Give yourself 120-second recharging sessions.

Sometimes we can't find an hour to do our favorite spoil-thyself-silly reward to perk ourselves back up. But we can always find a few spare minutes.

* * * * * * * * * * * * * * *

BOUNCE BACK ASSIGNMENT:

Do some yoga stretches. Call a friend. Sing a favorite song to yourself. Read something funny. Think of as many people you've kissed as you can—add in when and where. Check out your favorite website. Write in your blog.

Often even a mere 120 seconds can be enough to lift up your mood.

tip# **23**

Go with the flow.

𝕽emember when you were a kid and could work on a sand castle from the moment you hit the beach until it was time to go home? It was more than "playing." Your imagination was stimulated, your focus absolute. All that mattered was the task at hand. This is called "flow."

"People are seldom happier than when they are in the 'flow,'" says psychologist Mihaly Csikszentmihalyi, who has spent more than 25 years researching this phenomenon. He once described flow as "being completely involved in an activity for its own sake. The ego falls away. Time flies. Every action, movement, and thought follows inevitably from the previous one, like playing jazz. Your whole being is involved and you're using your skills to the utmost."

A lot of people experience flow while exercising. I know I do. As a runner, I often want to give up midway through my workout. But that's when I push myself through that wall of pain. I stay focused only on taking the next step, then the next step, then the next. Before I know it, I've completed my run. Athletes call it "being in the zone."

To be clear, flow is not about zoning out. Any damn fool can sit in front of the television and forget their troubles for an hour (or six). In fact, Csikszentmihalyi says that watching TV produces some of the lowest levels of satisfaction because it doesn't challenge people.

※　※　※　※　※　※　※　※　※　※　※　※　※　※　※　※

Bounce Back Assignment:

Find your flow. Seek out the thing that absorbs your attention utterly, the thing you look forward to, that takes your mind off your struggles, if only for a little bit. Flow can be illusive. If it was easy to get, we'd all be "flowing" all of the time. You may not find your flow right away, but keep looking for it. And when you do find it, make it a priority to fit flow into your daily life.

tip#

Get some ZZZZZZs.

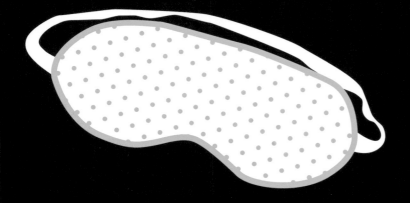

BOUNCE BACK ASSIGNMENT:

Try these insomnia busters.

* * * * * * * * * * * * * *

Meditate

Avoid Illuminated Alarm Clocks

Drink Herb Tea or Warm Milk

Don't Use Your Bed for TV or Reading

Don't Take Naps

Visualize Boring Things

Visualize Peaceful Things

Wake Up Earlier

Avoid Caffeine, Alcohol, and Tobacco

Exercise During the Day

Sleep Facing North

Pop a Tryptophan

tip# **25**

Create a balanced Wheel of Fortune.

If you're feeling totally thrown by a single bad event, take a closer look at your entire Wheel of Fortune. Never base your happiness on one thing. A status-y job. A hot bod. A sizzling paramour. Life is full of surprises. If you only have one thing bringing you happiness and it suddenly stops, then you'll feel as if your whole life has stopped.

FUN STUFF
ROMANCE
SPIRITUAL
FAMILY
WEALTH
CAREER
HEALTH
FRIENDS

✳ ✳ ✳ ✳ ✳ ✳ ✳ ✳ ✳ ✳ ✳ ✳ ✳ ✳

BOUNCE BACK ASSIGNMENT:

If your **Wheel of Fortune** were a real wheel, would it roll along smoothly…or would you be in for a bumpy ride? Consider which areas of your life you need to nurture to create a more well-rounded, consistent, balanced state of being.

tip# **26**

Watch out for hidden icebergs!

Okay. Admittedly, you've been through a very difficult time. But...

Are you viewing your tough circumstances with an accurate lens, or are you catastrophizing—blowing your situation out of proportion? It's easy to lose perspective when you're emotional. But why do we get so emotional in the first place?

"If you find yourself snowballing an unfortunate event into having dramatic, horrible consequences, this might be because you have an underlying 'iceberg belief,'" explains Dr. Karen Reivich, a professor at the University of Pennsylvania and coauthor of *The Resilience Factor*.

Iceberg beliefs are the thoughts that float beneath the surface of your consciousness: powerful forces that can significantly undermine your resilience and cause you to overreact to a particular situation. (Remember the *Titanic?*)

Iceberg beliefs begin forming in childhood and are often passed down from generation to generation like an ugly lamp.

Here are some typical ones:

1. "Things should always be fair."
2. "Women should never show their anger."
3. "Boys should not cry."
4. "Never let them know you are hurting."
5. "If you don't do it right, it isn't worth doing."
6. "People need to be appreciated for what they do."

Do any of these sound familiar? People's iceberg beliefs tend to fall into the areas of control, acceptance, and achievement, and they can really wreak havoc during a crisis by making you feel unbearably out of control, rejected, or a complete failure.

The best way to melt your iceberg beliefs is to use your adult-thinking mind to reevaluate them—just as you did a lot of other childhood beliefs.

"Your feelings are a result of your thinking," explains Dr. Reivich. "By changing the way you think, you can control your emotional reactions to stressful situations."

There's no question that shattering beliefs as strong and deeply seated as icebergs is no small task.

But think about the other things you used to believe:

1. "There is a very ugly monster living under my bed and he wants to eat me."

2. "There is nothing better than cake. Nothing."

3. "My parents know everything."

4. "My younger sibling is the worst thing that has ever happened to me."

5. "Kissing is G-R-O-S-S."

As we grow up, we change our mind about a lot of things. Why not our iceberg beliefs, too?

✳ ✳ ✳ ✳ ✳ ✳ ✳ ✳ ✳ ✳ ✳ ✳ ✳ ✳ ✳ ✳

Bounce Back Assignment:

Think about what your iceberg beliefs are. Write them down. Then next to each one, write a **PROOF OF INACCURACY.**

REMEMBER: If you can reprogram your thoughts, you can reprogram your emotions. It's not brainwashing, it's not even positive thinking. It's accurate thinking.

tip# 27

Throw out old
clothes and shoes,
and train your brain
to get rid of old
thoughts and ideas.

Psychologists believe you can trick your brain to feel more comfortable with change—by doing something like throwing out old clothes—and create a pro-change reaction to old outmoded ways of thinking.

The connection: You're learning to associate "change" with "fun" and the opportunity to make room for new, exciting things to come into your life.

You're learning that when you grow, you often "outgrow" and what worked for you in the past might need to be tossed in your present.

✳ ✳ ✳ ✳ ✳ ✳ ✳ ✳ ✳ ✳ ✳ ✳ ✳ ✳ ✳

Bounce Back Assignment:

Block out 30 minutes to go through your closet and remove old clothes and shoes that no longer become you. As you toss your dud duds aside, know you are preparing to **put aside old thoughts and beliefs that no longer fit who you are.**

tip#

Shrink that vacuum down to DustBuster size.

If you've experienced the loss of a job or a loved one, here are some tips for shrinking that huge vacuum left in your life down to DustBuster size.

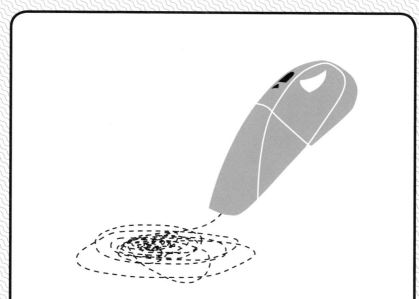

* * * * * * * * * * * * *

BOUNCE BACK ASSIGNMENT:

Get out your calendar **NOW,** and book up your days with doing more of **your "signature strengths,"** those things you're naturally talented at doing. Or maybe you have yet to discover your true signature strengths. If so, what are you waiting for? If you feel you have some untapped strengths, get them on tap today. Sign up for classes in these areas. Do it **now.** And by now, I mean **NOW.**

tip#

The sun not only helps plants thrive, but people, too.

Studies show 20% of Americans report feeling more depressed during winter months.

Scientists link this increase in depression to a decrease in sunlight. When sunlight decreases, we produce more melatonin, which makes us feel drowsy and anxious.

In contrast, studies show that in spring and summer, the sun's ultra-violet light frequencies serve bottomless nutrients to a human's biological, hormonal, and electrical systems.

Translation: Being in sunny weather literally creates a sunnier mood.

Another interesting finding was that patients with hospital beds by a sunny window had shorter stays than patients facing no window at all.

✳ ✳ ✳ ✳ ✳ ✳ ✳ ✳ ✳ ✳ ✳ ✳ ✳ ✳ ✳ ✳

Bounce Back Assignment:

Lighten up your mood with light. Go for a walk. Take a sunny vacation. Or brighten your home with full-spectrum bulbs, like Ott-Lite, Verilux, and GE's Reveal.

tip#

Time travel.

"Thinking happy thoughts literally creates a positive chemical change in the brain—which stimulates both positive physical and psychological benefits," says Deepak Chopra, in *Creating Health: How to Wake Up the Body's Intelligence*.

Chopra reports numerous studies in which people literally infused their brain and body with positive endorphins by time-traveling to happier times, thinking about happy memories from their past.

If you time-travel into the past or the future, and consciously think only about happy memories or optimistic goals, you can become both happier and healthier.

WARNING: Time-traveling to negative times creates the opposite effect! Sad thoughts have a negative impact on the body and overall brain chemistry. And unhappy, angry, hostile thoughts raise blood pressure, knot up the stomach, create a sluggish immune system, and can even bring on heart disease.

* * * * * * * * * * * * * * * *

Bounce Back Assignment:

Make a list of **five happy moments** and **five future goals** you're psyched about. Then, when you feel all is lost, enjoy a **Happy Mental Rental.** Close your eyes and think about this happy time. Envision everything about it. What are you wearing? How are you standing? What scent is in the air? The more sensual details, the stronger the neural connection, and the better the endorphin benefit.

tip# 31

You can be the mover of your own cheese.

After suffering from a really bad event, it's important to not get stuck in what's known as a "victim-head."

It felt particularly weird when I was too depressed to leave my apartment for months because I am normally an optimistic self-help book author, not some helpless twig…being tossed topsy and turvy in the winds of uncontrollable fate.

Egads! Is that melodramatic of me to write or what?

But that was exactly how I felt after the assault—out of control. I became anxiously aware that anything could happen to me at any time. And this sense of not being in control over my life created a dark despair within me.

This angst began to make more sense when, while researching resiliency, I discovered some interesting studies on autonomy.

The *Journal of Personality and Social Psychology* reported that the number-one contributor to well-being is not money, good looks, or popularity! No, the biggest life goodie is autonomy, defined as "the feeling that your life—its activities and habits—are self-chosen and self-endorsed."

Studies at the University of Michigan confirmed that "Having a strong sense of controlling one's life is a more dependable predictor of positive feelings of well-being than any other objective conditions of life."

In one famous study, researchers randomly gave mice either cheese or electric shocks. The mice did everything they could to avoid the shocks and get more cheese, but when they figured out that their actions had no effect, they lapsed into a state of passive listlessness.

When they were eventually given the choice (autonomy) to avoid the electric shocks or get more cheese, the mice were so bummed out they just lay there, choosing not to do anything at all!

Similarly (but with better results), psychologist Judith Rodin encouraged nursing home patients to exert more control in their lives by motivating them to make a few key changes to their environments (to decide if the air conditioning should be on or off or how furniture should be arranged). Rodin also pushed patients to request changes in various nursing home policies, which they subsequently received. As a result, 93% of these patients became more alert, active, and happy.

It just goes to show that, unlike a mouse, we Homo sapiens are lucky to have this thing called "consciousness." We know better than to give up, even after our autonomy has been challenged.

Right?

* * * * * * * * * * * * * * * * * *

BOUNCE BACK ASSIGNMENT:

If right now you're feeling so sideswiped that you're tempted to do nothing but lie around, sleep late, and watch TV—don't! Instead, increase your feeling of autonomy by increasing your **"internal locus of control,"** the power you have to make easy, small changes.

So today, create three deadlines for new projects and three exciting events to be shared with loved ones. Mark them all down on your calendar. Then do these things and meet these people in a timely, efficient way.

Establishing deadlines—then meeting them—will absolutely help you feel like the feisty, kick-ass master of your destiny that you know you are!

tip#

Think of life as a gigantic ice cream parlor with infinite flavors to taste.

BOUNCE BACK ASSIGNMENT:

Tell yourself the goal of life is to taste as many flavors of experiences as you can.

RECOGNIZE: Every challenge offers the opportunity to think **a new flavor of thought** and feel a new flavor of emotion. The more varied the flavors of life you get to taste, the more interesting, layered, educated, and world-experienced you'll be. Admittedly, you won't like every flavor. But hey, you don't need to go near that flavor ever again. Instead, indulge in flavors you know you're passionate about! And don't be afraid to taste something that might look funny—you never know!

tip# **33**

Stretch yourself.

Fact: You don't grow unless you stretch yourself.

Problem: Stretching usually means you feel (ugh) discomfort. You have to deal with the pain of the unknown and working new emotional and mental muscle groups.

Fact: Most people are (1) fearful of the unknown, (2) comfy with putting in the least effort, (3) not willing to put up with short-term pain for long-term gain.

Fact: But not you, right?

✳ ✳ ✳ ✳ ✳ ✳ ✳ ✳ ✳ ✳ ✳ ✳ ✳ ✳ ✳ ✳

Bounce Back Assignment:

During challenging times, remember: No growing **pain,** no growing **gain!** So don't forget to stretch.

tip#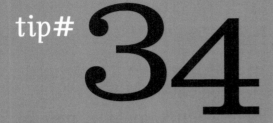

34

See it as it is and see
it as better than it is.

It's a funny thing, motivation.

Sometimes it's easier to motivate yourself to make a million dollars than a thousand dollars because you're so incredibly jazzed up by this lunatic loot, you have more energy to jump over obstacles in a single bound, even boundless bounds.

As you emerge from your Vortex, create the dreamiest of dream goals, and psych yourself up to try harder than ever to bounce back up.

Aaron Beck, a famed psychotherapist specializing in helping people stuck in depression, believes "hopelessness" is the key psychological factor that keeps people trapped in despair.

His solution? Dangle, dangle, dangle some extraordinary wonders to reach for!

✳ ✳ ✳ ✳ ✳ ✳ ✳ ✳ ✳ ✳ ✳ ✳ ✳ ✳ ✳ ✳

Bounce Back Assignment:

"WITHOUT A VISION, PEOPLE PERISH." Imagine a vision of how you want your life to be. Then imagine it 50% better than how you want it. Where do you see yourself in a year? Make it 50% even more amazing! Where do you see yourself in five years? Double your goals for joy! Get yourself into a totally psyched frame of mind so you can go out there and soar.

tip# **35**

Don't just write a "To Do" list.
Write a "To Be" list.

What kind of person will you have to become
to get through tough times and snag all you want in life?

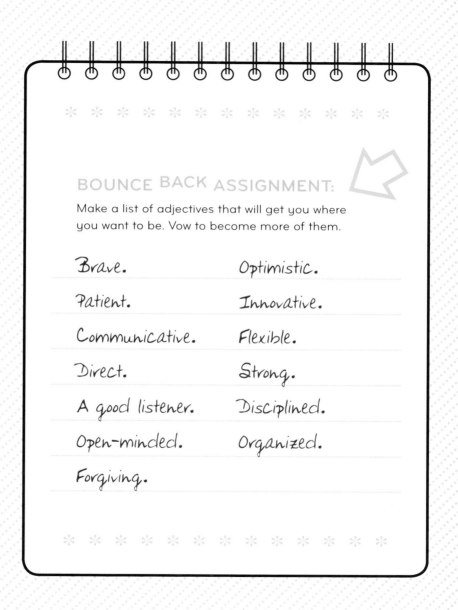

BOUNCE BACK ASSIGNMENT:

Make a list of adjectives that will get you where you want to be. Vow to become more of them.

Brave.	Optimistic.
Patient.	Innovative.
Communicative.	Flexible.
Direct.	Strong.
A good listener.	Disciplined.
Open-minded.	Organized.
Forgiving.	

tip# **36**

Real sugar creates real sugar blues.

Sugar blues is a real ailment, also clinically referred to as "Man, are you crabby!"

✳ ✳ ✳ ✳ ✳ ✳ ✳ ✳ ✳ ✳ ✳ ✳ ✳ ✳ ✳

BOUNCE BACK ASSIGNMENT:

During depression-prone times, cut back on obvious sugar-laden sweets like chocolate, cake, and alcoholic beverages as well as the nonobvious sugars found in high-carb items like pizza and pasta. Instead, satisfy your sweet tooth with fruits that break down more slowly so you can avoid the blood sugar spikes and falls.

tip#

Laughter is contagious good health.

When someone shares a good laugh with you, they are not only spreading joy but lowering blood pressure, boosting the immune system, improving brain functioning, lowering the risk of heart disease, as well as reducing depression, anger, anxiety, and stress.

A healthy sense of humor during hard times is especially beneficial not only for all these physical benefits, but the psyche as well.

You know the expression, "It only hurts when I laugh." I like to think, "It only hurts when I can't laugh."

For me, humor is a great "enlightening" agent—helping to shed light on an event, so it no longer appears as earthshaking. I have often quipped that comedy is when bad things happen to people who aren't me. One day I realized this joke of mine was actually very Buddhist. By removing my ego, I'm no longer personally connected to a situation's outcome or concerned about humiliation or self-pity. Thus it's a lot easier to see the humor in it.

When you have a good sense of humor, you are better able to reframe the meaning you give an event so it no longer appears so devastating or shameful.

❋ ❋ ❋ ❋ ❋ ❋ ❋ ❋ ❋ ❋ ❋ ❋ ❋ ❋ ❋ ❋

Bounce Back Assignment:

Pretend you are Jon Stewart, and put a funny spin on a bad event in your life. Recognize that a good belly laugh will not only make things feel less overwhelming, it will offer the opportunity for a more objective perspective.

If the #2 pencil is so popular, why is it still #2?

tip# 38

Give yourself a break to avoid a breakdown.

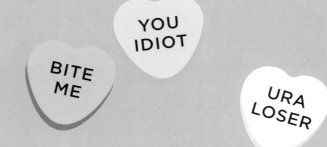

The Dalai Lama said, "If you want others to be happy, practice compassion. If you want to be happy, practice compassion."

In other words, don't pressure yourself to recover too fast.

After a traumatic event, time seems to move in slow motion. Each week will feel like seven. You feel trapped in limbo, where everything is out of your control.

Do not be impatient about your progress or impractical either.

Months after the event, you might think you should be feeling much better. But realize the healing process has no timetable. Trying to feel 100% better 100% of the time is unrealistic and will only lead to further disappointment.

After six months, even feeling 51% positive that things will get better and life is going to be okay is a huge milestone. Celebrate it. You have turned the corner of your depression!

✳   ✳   ✳   ✳   ✳   ✳   ✳   ✳   ✳   ✳   ✳   ✳   ✳   ✳   ✳   ✳

Bounce Back Assignment:

Have a **realistic expectation** for your speed of recovery. Come up with an **achievable** goal for feeling better, and take baby steps toward reaching it. Keep track of your progress by putting little **+** and **-** signs in your journal every time you feel positive or negative. Your goal is to eventually see a trend of more **+** signs!

tip# **39**

Shrink negativity into nuggetivity.

Limit the amount of time you allow yourself to think negative thoughts to 3-minute nuggets, three times a day.

* * * * * * * * * * * * * * *

BOUNCE BACK ASSIGNMENT:

Set aside a specific time of day when you will allow yourself to think negative thoughts. Then during the day, whenever a negative thought enters your head, tell yourself you can't think about it until **your preset Negativity Appointment.** Who knows, maybe you won't even want to think negatively once this time swings around.

Also, to further reduce negativity, **write** your thoughts on paper. **Get it out. Then cross it out.** As you put a line through the words, tell yourself you're letting go of these negative thoughts. **Then let go, dammit!**

~~I'm so depressed.~~

~~I hate my job.~~

~~I'm an idiot.~~

~~I can't do this.~~

tip#

Know your weak
times in a week.

BOUNCE BACK ASSIGNMENT:

Look at your calendar. Are there **days** of the week you know you feel better or worse? **When** do you feel most stressed? Are weekends harder? **Which** of your week's events or situations make you lose perspective? Are holidays, anniversaries, or birthdays emotional minefields? Know thyself and **plan ahead** for thyself. Make sure you have fun and calming things to do during Kryptonite times—as well as those Krypto-mornings and Krypto-late-afternoons!

tip# **41**

Use vacations as restorations.

Why is it that you often must go away to have important life realizations come a-knockin'? Yes, often the best way to see what's going on in your life is from a distance of a few thousand miles.

I have some theories on why a vacation is perfect for neuron renewal:

1. Getting away reminds you: Eureka! You are just one little microdot life in this humongous world, which means you don't have huge problems. You have microdot problems, which only YOU—and YOU ALONE—are in charge of fixing. So you can live the most amazing microdot life imaginable!

2. At least for the moment it takes to stare at that amazing painting, church, view, leather pocketbook, chocolate croissant, you're being fully mindful and in the now rather than obsessing about your past difficulties.

3. When you change your scenery, you change your thinking energy— and are more apt to see new solutions. You also remove potentially depressing visual triggers that might be keeping you stuck in a negative place.

4. Vacations keep you away from phones, newspapers, e-mail, and incoming bills. Duh! This liberation creates much inner celebration!

* * * * * * * * * * * * * * * *

Bounce Back Assignment:

Take a vacation—and leave your emotional baggage at the airport. If possible, go to a spot with lots of **sun,** thereby getting extra perks of light and exercise. While away, write yourself "in-sightseeing postcards" of your trip and mail them home. They will remind you of a perspective you don't want to lose.

tip# 42

See work failure as "fullure"—full of lessons.

If you've just endured a career adversity, join the crowd—and by the way, it's a very distinguished successful crowd. Many members of the Fortune 500 Club could easily earn membership in the Misfortune 500 Club.

Successful people are not people who never fail. They're people who know how to fail really, really well. If they fall on their faces, they use that leverage to push themselves up higher.

Bill Gates actually relishes the lessons of failure so much, he purposefully hires people at Microsoft who have made mistakes. "It shows that they take risks," says Gates.

Harvard business school professor John Kotter says it's more worrisome to executives if job applicants claim they've never failed—because this means they've never taken risks.

Roberto Goizueta, Coca-Cola's CEO, says the risk-taker mentality is the very reason he hired back the guy who launched New Coke—a huge marketing failure.

Goizueta recognized how you can become uncompetitive if you're not tolerant of mistakes. In fact, if you let "avoiding failure" become your motivator, you're going dangerously down the path of inactivity. "You can stumble only if you're moving," he says.

✳ ✳ ✳ ✳ ✳ ✳ ✳ ✳ ✳ ✳ ✳ ✳ ✳ ✳ ✳ ✳

Bounce Back Assignment:

Okay. So you stumbled and fell. Maybe even big-time. Focus on how your risky thinking makes you more **knowledgeable**. When being interviewed about your failure, own it as a **positive lesson**—proof you are a valuable outside-the-box thinker.

tip#

Time not only **heals,**
time **reveals.**

Now for a Buddhist tale . . .

There once was A Family who lived in The Village of You Never Know.

One day, The Only Son slipped on an orange while tilling soil—and broke his arm. His Mother and Father were distraught. How could this happen? How unlucky!

The next day…The Father slipped on an orange—and broke both his legs. Geez, this A Family felt hexed! They wondered: Why all this punishment?

Then within the week…A Big, Bad War broke out in The Village of You Never Know, and all the able-bodied men were called on to fight.

The Only Son and Father were deemed unsuitable soldiers due to their injuries and were left back home.

It was a doozy of a war. I won't go into NC-17 violent detail, but nobody came home. Nada a soldier.

Suddenly A Family didn't feel so put upon.

After getting a good eyeful of the Big Picture of Life, they even felt pretty lucky.

✳ ✳ ✳ ✳ ✳ ✳ ✳ ✳ ✳ ✳ ✳ ✳ ✳ ✳ ✳ ✳

Bounce Back Assignment:

Look at the big picture… Recognize that what looks bad close up might look pretty damn good from a distance.

tip# 44

hire a higher power.

$\mathfrak{I}$ **must confess,** I'm more spiritual than I am religious. And as far as praying to God goes, I'm more about looking inside for guidance—tapping into our own abundantly powerful inner resources—which some might say is where God resides.

Which reminds me of one of my favorite cartoons…Two sock puppets are talking to each other. One sock puppet says to the other, "Sometimes I wonder if there is a hand."

I believe we are our own inner hand, and that the godly power resides within each of us to create the lives we desire—no matter what the challenges!

That said, I also believe it doesn't matter where your "godly guidance" comes from—deep inside you or from high above. What does matter is that you take the time to seek it during times of trouble. Studies show that people who are involved in religion report less depression than those who are not religious. In one study, 101 students between ages 18 and 49 were asked to complete a survey about their religious practices. Those who went to church regularly and prayed often were the ones who scored the highest in happiness.

Personally, I think there's a reason why those religious people scored high on the happiness meter—and not all those reasons have to do with religion per se. Religious people benefit from the guaranteed social support that can be found in a church, synagogue, or mosque. And this community is especially helpful during a trauma or crisis.

Plus, religion can provide a sense of meaning and purpose. According to psychiatrist Ed Diener, having a belief in something bigger than yourself—a sense of order amid all the chaos—is a vital ingredient to happiness.

You can find this meaning in religious prayer or a spiritual belief system. Or you can simply develop a personal life philosophy that inspires you to seek lessons and growth.

That said, I gotta confess: It was hard for me to consider hiring a higher power in the midst of my Vortex.

I kept thinking, Where was God when I needed him/her that day of my sexual assault? If God did exist, He was, as German philosopher Gottfried Leibniz claimed, "an underachiever." In Leibniz's writings he—like so many of us when going through a personal tragedy—wondered how a God who was supposedly good could allow so much evil and suffering in the world!

In the end, Leibniz came to God's defense, theorizing that because God was all knowing, He could evaluate all the possibilities of various worlds. And so perhaps God chose the world we're in—as bad as it might seem at times—because it offered the least possible evil.

In other words: No matter how challenging your life might feel, it could have been a whole lot worse. That comforted me a bit.

Rabbi Harold Kushner's view on why bad things might happen to good people also comforted me. Kushner's basic belief: God could have controlled everything about our lives—the good and the bad. But then we'd merely be Stepford humans and there'd be no fun in living at all—and no growth either. Hence God granted us this fabulous perk called "free will," which also means we have a choice in how we cope with any suffering we are dealt in the process of all our "free will" living!

BOUNCE BACK ASSIGNMENT:

If during a time of loss or suffering, you would like to **seek meaning and purpose** but are overwhelmed by doubt and hopelessness, I recommend this warm-up psalm for your psyche. I'd heard this when I was a kid, then found it again by coincidence on Google after the assault. (Hmmm... unless it wasn't sheer coincidence!?)

✳ ✳ ✳ ✳ ✳ ✳ ✳ ✳ ✳ ✳ ✳ ✳

A PSALM FOR YOUR PSYCHE
(repeat as often as necessary!):

I asked for strength...
And God gave me Difficulties to make me strong.

I asked for wisdom...
And God gave me Problems to solve.

I asked for prosperity...
And God gave me a Brain and Brawn to work.

I asked for courage...
And God gave me Danger to overcome.

I asked for love...
And God gave me Troubled people to help.

I asked for favors...
And God gave me Opportunities.

I received nothing I wanted
but I received everything I needed.

tip#

On the spiritual
path, the bigger your
misfortunes, the bigger
the compliment.

In Buddhism, huge difficulties are thought to be a compliment—a sign you're an old soul being tested to see if you're ready to rise to the next level toward enlightenment.

The Law of Karma also suggests that whatever happens to us in this life is tailored specifically for us as lessons to be learned. And although many of our life exams might feel very difficult at times, the universe knows what it's up to and never gives us more than we can handle learning.

❋ ❋ ❋ ❋ ❋ ❋ ❋ ❋ ❋ ❋ ❋ ❋ ❋ ❋ ❋ ❋

Bounce Back Assignment:

View present bad events as a **test** of your character. Now ask yourself, What the heck are you being tested for? Patience? Compassion? Improved communication? Resilience? Forgiveness? Open-mindedness? What **strengths** must you develop further? Now consciously go out there and **develop** them!

tip#46

Create an elevator pitch
of your story to keep
your spirits high.

"**After you've been through a trauma or large loss,** assume that people won't be good listeners," says Dr. Al Siebert, director of Portland, Oregon's Resiliency Center and author of *The Resiliency Advantage.* The average person will listen to you talk about your ordeal for 1 to 2 minutes tops, before they want to get away or interrupt you with their opinion. This can be really hurtful and emotionally stressful when you're in a place of vulnerability.

Siebert suggests you protect your spirit by constructing some boundaries, and coming up with a 1- to 2-minute preplanned way to describe what you went through—an elevator pitch of sorts. He also reminds us that it's very okay to decide not to share anything at all. You can simply tell people directly, "Thanks for asking, but I don't care to talk about it right now."

* * * * * * * * * * * * * * * * *

Bounce Back Assignment:

Figure out what you want your 1- to 2-minute story to be. Try to use neutral or positive language so you don't keep reliving your pain. Also, Siebert recommends putting a **positive "kicker"** at the end. For example, **"Yes, I've been through a horrible time, but I'm handling it okay. How about you? Have you ever been through anything like this?"** Requesting empathy makes it less likely that your listener's response will hurt or disappoint you.

If you feel you're with someone supportive with whom you want to share the experience, check in with your listener first, saying something like, "I must confess what I went through is a very emotional experience. If you have an hour, I'd love to share it with you." That way you guard against the disappointment of having your tale curtailed.

tip# 47

View yet as yes.

Remember: Just because a bad event might be creating a block between what you want and what you have, this doesn't mean you won't eventually make the world say yes to you. The universe's delays are not the universe's denials.

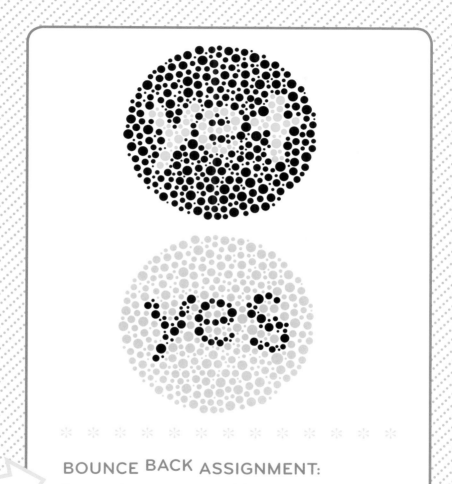

BOUNCE BACK ASSIGNMENT:

Envision what you want on a delivery truck coming toward you—just stuck for a bit in traffic.

tip#

Bonsai you? Or mighty oak you? It's your pickeroo.

Every seven years, every cell in the human body will change completely, be gone, pffffft. Yet every seven years, you always miraculously wake up You. How is that possible?

According to Aristotle, it's because inside you is your "entelechy"—your original "You Seed." Just as an oak seed is destined to always grow into an oak tree—and is never to become a petunia plant, a rosebush, or an umbrella—you too have your internal seed, ensuring you will always grow into a You of some variety.

But depending on its environment, an oak seed can grow into a Mighty Oak or a stunted Bonsai Oak. So, too, Aristotle warns, you might grow into a Mighty Human Being or get stunted into a Bonsai Human Being depending on how you weather stormy circumstances.

Actually, Aristotle believed that stormy events were exactly what helped humans to grow stronger, in the same way trees that endure the stormiest conditions are the ones with the strongest branches.

Stormy times give us the opportunity to grow into Mightier Human Beings, provided we focus on the big picture rather than on our difficulties, said Aristotle. "It concerns us," he wrote, "to know the purposes we seek in life, for then, like archers aiming at a definite mark, we shall be more likely to attain what we want."

✳ ✳ ✳ ✳ ✳ ✳ ✳ ✳ ✳ ✳ ✳ ✳ ✳ ✳ ✳ ✳

Bounce Back Assignment:

Like an archer, **stay focused** on your purpose in life. Every time you're tempted to see only the pain and sorrow right in front of you, repeat the words **"Mighty Growth"** and take aim.

tip# 49

"The voyage of true discovery lies not in seeking new landscapes, but in **seeing with new eyes."**

—MARCEL PROUST

If you've just undergone a very distressing experience, try switching your lens on the world.

Okay! Here's a quickie Buddhist tale to confound and inspire!

One day a very wealthy man took his son on a trip to the country to live a few days on a farm with a very poor family. His goal: Teach his son a lesson about what it means to be poor.

Upon their return, the father asked his son, "So, what did you learn about what it means to be poor?"

The son answered, "I learned that we have one dog. They have four. We have a pool that reaches to the middle of our garden. They have a creek with no end. We have imported lanterns. They have an abundance of stars at night. We have a small piece of land to live on. They have fields that go beyond sight. We buy our food. They grow theirs. We have walls around our property. They have friends to protect them."

The boy's father was speechless.

"Yes, Dad," said the son, "you showed me how poor WE truly are."

The lesson to be learned: With an open mind— "new eyes"—you can create a new reality.

✳ ✳ ✳ ✳ ✳ ✳ ✳ ✳ ✳ ✳ ✳ ✳ ✳ ✳ ✳ ✳ ✳

Bounce Back Assignment:

Today, stop reacting in the same old ways to whatever is getting you upset. Try viewing your life with **"new eyes."**

tip# 50

What goes down
often bounces
back even higher.

⚠ WARNING: Obstacles to **joy** appear larger than they are during a **crisis.**

Just as the rich get richer, studies show that often the happy get happier and the sad get sadder—because of simmering brain temperatures—also known as "resonance."

Happy thoughts all share the same resonance in the brain—and are shown to naturally attract the memory of other happy thoughts—also simmering at the same happy "resonance."

Chances are you've witnessed this theory of resonance with guitars. You know if you pluck the G string on one guitar, the G string on any nearby guitar will have "sympathetic resonance" and start to vibrate as well! If you haven't experienced this, check it out! It's very cool.

Well, memories are "tuned in" at specific frequencies, based on the information they're encoded with—like "this is high-level happy stuff" or "this is low-level miserable stuff."

Whatever resonance your present thoughts are simmering at ("high-level happy" or "low-level miserable"), they'll attract memories of similar information.

The result: When you're happy, a stream of positive thoughts ensues. Ditto on simmering negative thoughts.

The good news: Over time, negative brain resonances eventually simmer back up to their normal, daily, even-keeled levels. When they do, that's when the feeling of "rebounding" kicks in.

So if lately you've been worried that you're never going to feel like your normal self again, don't. You are biologically wired to return to your normal general happiness level.

Professor Richard Lucas, at Michigan State University, researched the effects of bad and good times on mood permanence. He focused on a wide range of people: from folks who won huge amounts of money to those who experienced debilitating injuries. His research showed all people initially reacted strongly to the good or bad in their lives. However, eventually nearly everyone returned to their former set happiness zone.

More good news: His studies showed that after distressing times, many people actually reported rebounding to a higher-than-usual good mood. He attributes this bounce-back-higher effect to people appreciating the good in their life after suffering the bad.

The result: Your renewed focus on all the positive things in your life retrieves even more simmering positive thought memories…and upward your mood does go!

BOUNCE BACK ASSIGNMENT:

Create a **Gratitude Journal.** Record: Who do you love? What do you love? What do you love to do? Psychologists find that people who keep weekly gratitude journals end up feeling happier, more energetic, and more optimistic than those who don't. So write down those people, things, and experiences that bring you joy, and keep your brain resonating at a happy temperature.

tip# 51

Anger is a boomerang.

In fact, anger is so much of a boomerang, we could rename it "boomeranger."

During challenging times, it's easy to rage against the world—and specific people in it. But you can be sure that the anger you send out will come back at you and make you feel even worse.

Anger is a powerful emotion that manifests itself in lots of sneaky ways.

When I spoke about my sexual assault, many of my friends would say, "Come on, Karen! You must be so pissed off at that guy." But as far as I could tell, I wasn't. I truly didn't feel the sensation of anger within me. I just felt very sad and very hungry. As I keep mentioning, I had this never-ending urge to eat chocolate.

Turns out I wasn't hungry. I was furious! According to many psychologists I've spoken with since, my urge to devour chocolate was my way of acting out my anger—raging at myself and my thighs—instead of at my assaulter and his kneecaps.

Apparently, this is not unusual behavior for women.

According to Dr. Sandra Thomas, psychologist and editor of *Women and Anger,* because so many women are uncomfortable expressing anger outwardly, they often turn it inward, transferring their rage into substance abuse.

Whether a woman is abusing drugs or chocolate, she tends to fall into an unfortunate downward spiraling of self-esteem because she's not only angry about her ordeal but upset about her addiction.

Talk about a raw deal. But it's not like men have it any easier.

For many men, powerful emotions that make them feel vulnerable, like heartbreak or failure, often manifest themselves as rage. Remember when I said that anger is sneaky? That's because it tricks you into feeling empowered. Rage feels strong. Grief, loss, and failure feel weak.

I was surprised by how many of my male friends actually offered to perform violent acts against my assaulter. I'm still not sure how serious they were, but it was clear these guys were offering up their "projected anger" as a way to express empathy.

The bottom line is that, male or female, we all struggle with ways to deal with our anger. As Dr. Thomas reminds us, "Anger is like a squeezed balloon. If it does not come out in one way, it will in another."

Psychologists at the University of Wisconsin have come to believe that anger is the number-one trigger for substance abuse. They've developed a method called **"forgiveness therapy" that helps patients find ways to release the rage that is at the root of their substance abuse.** And it seems to be working.

In one study, 14 patients with drug and alcohol dependence were randomly assigned either a twice-weekly forgiveness therapy session or routine drug/alcohol therapy treatment. Guess what? The participants in forgiveness therapy showed significantly more improvement than those who only did routine drug/alcohol treatment.

Bottom line: When you are feeling angry after a trauma or loss, it is essential that you get in touch with your anger and express it appropriately. Only then will you find forgiveness and closure.

✳ ✳ ✳ ✳ ✳ ✳ ✳ ✳ ✳ ✳ ✳ ✳ ✳

BOUNCE BACK ASSIGNMENT:

Release your rage in healthy ways: Punch a sofa cushion; scream into a pillow; rip a newspaper to shreds; run in place; throw a safe breakable object; stomp your feet. Do whatever it takes to get the anger out of your system (at least for a little bit).

Now, take a deep breath and try this **forgiveness therapy exercise** developed by anger expert and psychologist Everett Worthington. With a little work (and a lot of courage), you may find a more permanent release for your anger:

A. Recall the hurt.

B. Empathize and try to understand the act from the perpetrator's perspective.

C. Be altruistic by recalling a time you were forgiven.

D. Put your forgiveness into words— in a letter to be sent or never sent.

E. Don't dwell.

tip# 52

Do antidote thought therapy.

𝔐any people going through a Vortex do affirmations, but I've found that "Antidote Thought Therapy" is more effective.

Here's how it works: Remember back to a fabulous time—perhaps when you slam-dunked a project or received incredible amounts of love and admiration.

Now narrow down these thoughts into one or two powerful words like:

SLAM DUNK   STAR   **LOVE ORB**   SEXUAL MAGNET

These will be your Antidote Words whenever a depressing or disempowering thought enters your mind.

Antidote Thought Therapy works more powerfully on your mind because it is linked to facts of past success, and therefore penetrates your troublemaking subconscious more readily.

❊ ❊ ❊ ❊ ❊ ❊ ❊ ❊ ❊ ❊ ❊ ❊ ❊ ❊ ❊ ❊

Bounce Back Assignment:

Next time a negative feeling enters your mind, zap it with your Antidote Words.

tip# **53**

Crises can deplete
your health.

In fact, depression is a "whole-body disorder"—having deleterious effects on the heart, brain, bones, and metabolism.

BOUNCE BACK ASSIGNMENT:

Make sure you don't overdraw vitamins, minerals, and serotonin. **For better mood, vitality, and relaxation, try:**

St. John's Wort

Ginkgo

B_{12}

Folic Acid

Vitamin C

Calcium

Zinc

Flaxseed

Magnesium

Calcium

B_6

tip#

Spooning is good medicine.

To test the power of cuddling on reducing distress, researchers at the University of North Carolina's Department of Psychiatry had one group of speakers receive hugs and cuddles before a public speaking event, and another group who did not. The speakers who didn't get the tender lovin' cuddles had much higher heart rates and blood pressures than speakers who did.

Indeed, many hospitals recognize the soothing power of touch and now include postoperative massage in their recuperative therapies.

As a psychiatrist who has worked with molested and raped individuals, Dr. Mark Goulston notes that people who have been through a physical violation might especially benefit from some positive, tender cuddling.

"I have become convinced that our skin has a memory separate from our minds—of good touch, bad touch, and no touch," explains Dr. Goulston. "There is not enough good touch in the world, and too many people walk around settling for no touch, in an effort to avoid bad touch."

If your physical boundaries have been violated, it's especially important to seek out loving touch so you can ultimately shed your skin's negative memory and get more in sync with positive touch sensations once again.

✳ ✳ ✳ ✳ ✳ ✳ ✳ ✳ ✳ ✳ ✳ ✳ ✳ ✳ ✳

Bounce Back Assignment:

No matter how down you feel, find someone you **trust** and feel safe enough with to cuddle up. Even a **hug** or two from a platonic buddy can boost your mood. Don't be shy about requesting a hug. Remember, it's a win/win of stress reduction and increased comfort for both the hugger and hugee. **Another cuddle option:** Go to a pet store and hold a few puppies.

tip# 55

Sing your heartache out.

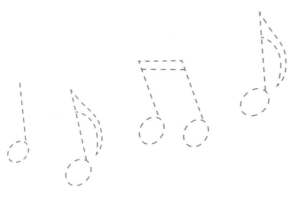

The Institute of Music, Health and Education has found that just 5 minutes of singing or humming can put you in a sunnier mood.

The cathartic power of music and singing has been recognized for eons. Aristotle claimed: "When (people) have made use of the melodies which fill the soul with orgiastic feeling, they are brought back…to a normal condition as if they had been medically treated."

Various religions throughout time have recognized how music helps people transcend dark emotions. Indeed religious leaders from around the world—who often can't agree on much of anything—all concur on the cathartic power of music on the mind, spirit, and body.

Today, established health care professionals called **music therapists** actually prescribe treatments of singing, dancing, and listening to music as a method to help people heal from trauma or difficult circumstances.

A strong believer in music therapy, Dr. Oliver Sacks reports in *Awakenings* how music therapy provides an outlet for people who are otherwise withdrawn and uncommunicative and helps ease the trauma of grieving.

Some of my personally recommended musical boosters:

"WE WILL ROCK YOU" QUEEN	**"I CAN SEE CLEARLY NOW"** BOB MARLEY
"DANCING QUEEN" ABBA	**"CALLING ALL ANGELS"** K.D. LANG
"I WILL SURVIVE" GLORIA GAYNOR	**"IN MY LIFE"** THE BEATLES
"MOCKINGBIRD" CARLY SIMON & JAMES TAYLOR	**"BANANA BOAT SONG"** HARRY BELAFONTE
"LIKE A PRAYER" MADONNA	**"GIRLS JUST WANNA HAVE FUN"** CYNDI LAUPER
"MUSTANG SALLY" WILSON PICKETT	**"BRASS IN POCKET"** PRETENDERS
"THESE BOOTS ARE MADE FOR WALKIN'" NANCY SINATRA	**"EMOTIONAL RESCUE"** ROLLING STONES

"SIMPLY THE BEST" TINA TURNER	**"MY WAY"** FRANK SINATRA
"LIKE A ROLLING STONE" BOB DYLAN	**"LIVIN' ON A PRAYER"** BON JOVI
"RESPECT" ARETHA FRANKLIN	**"WE ARE THE CHAMPIONS"** QUEEN

A5 A7 B5 B7 C5 C7

✳ ✳ ✳ ✳ ✳ ✳ ✳ ✳ ✳ ✳ ✳ ✳ ✳

Bounce Back Assignment:

When in the shower or bath, **sing out your heart's content.** Avoid songs once shared with an ex or lyrics that verge on the maudlin. If none of my recommended songs cheers you up, try singing, "Do You Know the Muffin Man…The Muffin Man… The Muffin Man…" Hey—it's hard to feel sad when you're singing this giddy tune. **Don't scoff. Try it.**

tip# **56**

What you're going through is not only human— it's reptilian.

Tongue-tied. Choked-up. Speechless.

During my Vortex mode I felt totally at a loss for words, unable to express myself. Yes, me—a writer and a talk-show host. As it turned out, there was a neurological explanation for my muteness.

During times of extreme stress, we humans cross over into what's called "distress" and revert to our primitive (reptilian) "fight, flight, or freeze" responses. The neurochemicals our bodies release while in this survival state take away nearly 80% of our ability to think.

Yikes! An 80% inefficiency of the brain! That's a lot of brain ineffi-ciency—especially considering we normally have three fabulous parts of brain circuitry to tap into:

1. The brain stem, or the reptilian "fight or flight or freeze" brain, which is focused on survival.

2. The limbic system, or the "emotional" (right) brain, which is focused on feelings.

3. The neocortex, or the "rational" (left) brain, which is focused on thinking, problem solving, and goal creation.

Dr. Mark Goulston, who has worked with suicidal teens and trained FBI and police hostage negotiators, knows all about bouncing back from challenging situations. "When you're in full distress mode, you lose your ability to think from either your neocortex or your limbic system. As a result, you can't express feelings or interpret events clearly so you revert to your 'reptile brain' seeking fight (in the form of anger). Or flight (in the form of addictions or solitude). Or freeze (in the form of denial or numbness)."

Neuroscientists have witnessed how differently the brain works during trauma by studying SPECT (single-photon emission computed tomography) scans, which measure blood flow and functional activity in the brain. For example, when a nontraumatic memory is induced in a Vietnam veteran, the brain synapses are shown to fire equally on both RIGHT and LEFT hemispheres and back and forth to each other. However, when a traumatic flashback is induced, the brain's RIGHT hemisphere—where images, vision, and emotions originate—becomes extremely active while the LEFT side of the brain—where speech and logic exist—completely shuts down.

The lessons to be learned:

1. Trauma memories are stored differently than ordinary memories and have a harder time being consciously understood and processed.

2. There are neurological reasons why people undergoing trauma feel tongue-tied, choked-up and speechless. The left brain hemisphere is literally being locked out.

"What ultimately heals people," says Goulston, "is the ability to integrate all three of the circuitries of the brain." And he has devised the following exercise to help you do that.

* * * * * * * * * * * * * * * *

Bounce Back Assignment:

If you're having a hard time talking and thinking clearly after a trauma, Goulston recommends that you close your eyes, visually recall your experience, then follow these six steps for "walking" your way up from your lowest level reptile brain to your **highest rational neocortex:**

STEP 1: **Become Physically Aware.** What are your physical reactions to distress?

ANSWER: I feel _____ (tense, tight, numb, nauseated, etc.) in my _____ (stomach, neck, head, back, etc.).

You start here because most people feel stress in a place they can name. (And being able to come up with the correct answer to an exercise increases motivation to continue!)

STEP 2: Become Emotionally Aware. What are the emotions that most closely fit with your physical sensations?

ANSWER: I feel _____ (angry, afraid, uptight, depressed, etc.). Recent research by Matthew Lieberman at UCLA shows that simply being able to name an emotion halves your "amygdala activation," otherwise known as your emotionality. So this step should calm you by 50%.

STEP 3: Become Aware of Your Impulses. What do your feelings make you want to do?

ANSWER: I have this uncontrollable urge to _____ (run, attack, blame, make an excuse, feel sorry for myself, withdraw, etc.). Being able to translate a named emotion into a named impulse is the beginning of insight, which means you're already starting to tap into your neocortex.

STEP 4: Become Aware of Consequences. What might be the results if you acted on your impulses?

ANSWER: The negative consequences of my impulsive actions will be _____ (fall off my diet, stop exercising, get sick, lose my job, beat up on myself afterward, etc.).

STEP 5: **Become Aware of Alternate Solutions.** What would be a better thing to do right now?

ANSWER: Some positive, thoughtful actions I might take are _____ (do volunteer work, work on a project that excites me, exercise, call friends, etc.).

STEP 6: **Become Aware of Benefits.** Identify what you'll be getting by acting on the solution in step 5. Then sit back, breathe deeply, and remind yourself of the universal perks you'll receive now that you've tapped back into all three brain circuitries:

1. You will feel empowered to deal with challenges instead of avoiding them.

2. You will gain the respect of others and yourself.

3. You will dare to have goals for a happy life and pursue them.

tip#

Meditation can
work like medication
to calm you.

✳ ✳ ✳ ✳ ✳ ✳ ✳ ✳ ✳ ✳ ✳ ✳ ✳ ✳ ✳

BOUNCE BACK ASSIGNMENT:

Close your eyes. Become aware of your breath. **Exhale** the past. **Feel** it leaving your body. **Inhale** the future. **Envision** what you want coming toward you. Repeat until relaxed.

tip#
58

Cultivate the habit
of zest.

Remember how in the film *American Beauty* the young boy appreciates the beauty of an ordinary plastic bag blowing in the wind? He had what Bertrand Russell, author of *The Conquest of Happiness,* calls "the habit of zest."

People who cultivate the habit of zest are those who regularly take a lively interest in the most mundane of everyday moments and see the extraordinary in the ordinary.

Nobel Prize winner and scientist Daniel Kahneman says we experience about 20,000 individual moments in a day, each "moment" lasting only a few seconds. Whenever you retain a memory, it's because you were appreciating that single moment in time—and were able to freeze-frame it.

I believe the more memories you have, the more you are "living in the NOW." And the fewer memories you have, the more you are fast-forwarding through life.

* * * * * * * * * * * * * * * *

Bounce Back Assignment:

Cultivate the habit of zest. Purposefully **seek out the beauty in the seemingly trivial.** Walt Whitman saw a world of beauty in **"a leaf of grass."** Notice the colors and shapes of the foods you eat. The shadows a vase makes on the table. The interesting faces of the people on the bus with you. Not only will you experience a richer present, but a month from now you will be able to look back and have more happy memories to appreciate.

tip# **59**

Sometimes you gotta step outside yourself to remove yourself from a dark mood.

There are three paths to happiness, according to Martin Seligman: the pleasant life, the good life, and the meaningful life.

"The pleasant life" is basic moment-to-moment contentment—doing simple things like downing martinis or playing computer games. But eventually, you'll get bored and want more.

"The good life" comes through "engagement": spending time with friends and family or getting involved with a rewarding work project. This is a step-up on the happiness food chain.

But the biggest feelings of happiness come from leading "a meaningful life"—using personal strengths to serve some larger end.

In an experiment called "Philanthropy versus Fun," Seligman divided up his psychology students so that one group engaged in pleasurable activities (going to the movies, eating yummy ice cream) and the other group did philanthropic activities (volunteering at a soup kitchen, reading to the blind).

Guess what? The happiness afterglow of the fun was nothing compared to the lasting happiness of doing altruistic acts.

Meaning? Doing good for others will make you feel good—and, according to Seligman, your highest level of feel-good.

My guess: Altruism raises your mood because it raises your self-esteem, which increases happiness. Plus giving to others gets you outside of yourself and distracts you from your problems.

* * * * * * * * * * * * * * *

Bounce Back Assignment:

Ask yourself: What loving deed can I do? How can I help those in greater need? Consider getting involved with a charity where you can make an ongoing contribution.

tip# **60**

See awful as aweful.

Instead of viewing bad times as downright awful events, look at them as uplifting "awe-ful" events. Be curious and open to seeing an invisible order in the complicated machine called the universe. As Rumi said, "Sell your cleverness, purchase bewilderment." *Acquire more wonder—and life will feel more wonderful.*

awful

aweful

BOUNCE BACK ASSIGNMENT:

Say to yourself, **"Isn't it interesting how things are unfolding?"**
Pretend your story is a fascinating movie. What does the
protagonist need to learn? Maybe you're meant to end the
relationship you're in because this person is overly controlling—
like your mother was. And you're meant to finally put an end
to allowing overly controlling people into your life.

tip#

A dog is more than
a man's **best friend.**
It's a man's
best therapist.

$\mathcal{D}$ogs give more than unconditional love—they give companionship, lower blood pressure, and relief from stress. During Vortex mode, those are some very helpful treats a pet can fetch you! Tests have shown that walking a dog, or just having one as a companion, helps speed recovery from an illness and aids in rehabilitative efforts, writes Toyoharu Kojima in *Legacy of the Dog*.

Journalist Elizabeth Scott reports on an interesting study of a group of hypertensive New York stockbrokers, half of whom were given dogs and the other half weren't. Those who had dogs were found to have lower blood pressure and heart rates than those who didn't.

Other treats that doggies bring us: *more exercise and socialization.* Think about it. When you go for a walk with a dog, you are in the sun, breathing fresh air, getting your body's circulation going, attracting potential conversation—all of which increases overall good feelings big-time.

✳ ✳ ✳ ✳ ✳ ✳ ✳ ✳ ✳

Bounce Back Assignment:

Swap kvetching for fetching. Consider getting a pet or borrowing one. If it's a walkable critter like a dog (or ferret!), take it outside for a stroll. If it's more of an indoor buddy, lie down on the bed with the pet and cuddle for about 30 minutes— for some restorative pet therapy.

tip#

62

Change your **body.**
Change your **mind.**

When you're depressed, your body expresses it—your head and shoulders are slumped and your breathing shallow.

However, according to self-help guru Anthony Robbins, if you simply stand taller, pull your shoulders back, and punctuate your words with hand gestures, you will automatically feel a change in biochemistry and perk up.

"Emotion is created by motion," says Robbins. "The way you move changes the way you think and feel."

Robbins suggests that when you are going through hard times, consciously try to straighten your back, stretch more, take plenty of deep breaths, and walk more briskly.

Even a small thing like making yourself smile creates an increase of oxygen and blood flow that stimulates a more positive chemistry in the brain.

Actually, smiling takes less facial muscle effort than frowning. So because it's literally easier to smile than frown—smile, dammit!

* * * * * * * * * * * * * * * *

Bounce Back Assignment:

"Act" your way to a more **positive mood.** Start making more energetic, physical motions—and soon you'll feel more energetic, positive emotions!

tip# **63**

Watch how you **pepper** your conversations.

Psychologists say that a single trauma will strike you twice. Once in reality (the ordeal itself) and once in your mind (when you think about it and talk about it with others). Although there's nothing you can do about what happened to you, you *can* be mindful of the way you describe the trauma to yourself and to others.

Boris Cyrulnik, a famed French ethologist, says there's good reason to watch what you say. Almost all the women he's worked with who have experienced sexual trauma said it was not compassion that inspired them to recover. It was being told by others that they were "strong" that made them become strong. Cyrulnik argues that if someone expresses too much pity or horror for you, their view can actually escalate your pain.

I can relate. While in my Vortex I only wanted to be around people who reinforced my identity as a strong person—because I wasn't feeling so strong at the time.

Cyrulnik warns that **after a trauma, you need to make sure you don't talk with folks who accidentally keep you in "victim mode" by having you relive traumatic memories with depression-inducing language.**

Knowing the subliminal power of words, Morrie and Arleah Shectman, psychotherapists who specialize in bereavement counseling, use empowering language when helping people through a trauma. Morrie says he never talks "sympathetically" with his patients because it's disempowering and keeps patients coddled in victim mode. They get stuck reliving and examining their feelings rather than moving on.

Morrie is practicing what's called neurolinguistic programming (NLP) by priming his clients' subconscious mind with language that keeps them feeling strong. NLP is a therapy that believes you can influence the subconscious to change behaviors to more positive ones by consciously using positive language and by refocusing on those things in your control to change.

NLP is a pretty amazing phenomenon. In 2000, researcher John Bargh set up the now-famous study that showed how our linguistic context strongly affects our behavior.

Bargh gave two different groups of people two different lists of words to unjumble, telling them they were being tested on simple problem solving. The first list contained words suggesting impatience, rudeness, and aggressiveness; the second list had words suggesting patience, politeness, and calm. After the "test" was completed, the participants were asked to bring the lists to an administrator who was deep in conversation with a colleague—and THIS was when the true experiment took place.

All the participants given the list of words suggesting rudeness and aggressiveness *became those exact words,* angrily interrupting the administrator. However, of the participants primed with language suggesting patience and calm, the majority—82%!—never interrupted the administrator at all.

The lesson to be learned: The words we use and hear are powerful!

During your recovery avoid talking too much about the trauma itself, and instead **pepper your conversations, therapy sessions, and journal writing with strong, uplifting, optimistic words**—to keep you aimed in a strong, positive direction!

✳ ✳ ✳ ✳ ✳ ✳ ✳ ✳ ✳ ✳ ✳ ✳ ✳ ✳ ✳ ✳

Bounce Back Assignment:

I am a real believer in calling on a professional to help you with your recovery (see Tip #12). But when hiring a therapist, please be alert to the language the therapist uses—and the frequency with which he or she demands you describe your ordeal.

Of course this awareness should be applied across the board with friends and family. **YOUR GOAL:** Create a chorus around you that sings, "You are strong! You are strong!" in an endless loop of support!

tip# **64**

Learn how to ride
the elephant.

"**Controlling the mind is a lot like riding an elephant,**" says Dr. Jonathan Haidt, author of *The Happiness Hypothesis.* "The elephant represents the powerful thoughts and feelings—mostly unconscious—that drive your behavior. Humans, although much weaker, can exert control over the elephant, just as we exert control over negative thoughts and feelings."

To control your elephant, you must identify behaviors that get it feeling twitchy and thunderous. Are you kicking your elephant because you're not recovering fast enough? Are you nagging him with upsetting, pessimistic ruminations—you know, going over and over something in an attempt to make sense of it? When bad things happen, it's natural to overanalyze and obsess.

But rumination keeps you stuck. As Albert Einstein said, "We can't solve problems by using the same kind of thinking we used when we created them." To move forward, you need to switch mental tracks.

"Continually mulling over failure creates chronic stress," warns psychologist Everett Worthington. "Rumination is the number-one mental health bad boy; it's associated with obsessive-compulsive disorder, depression, anxiety and probably hives, too."

✳ ✳ ✳ ✳ ✳ ✳ ✳ ✳ ✳ ✳ ✳ ✳ ✳ ✳ ✳ ✳

Bounce Back Assignment:

Buy a journal. Write on the front: **ELEPHANT RETRAINING JOURNAL.** Every time you kick your elephant with a negative thought, write it down. After a week, look at your list. Notice anything? Are the same three (or 10) thoughts coming up again and again? Use the ABC technique in Tip #9 to dispute those thoughts and make your elephant a gentler beast.

tip#

Enter the Identity Protection Program.

What you get in life all depends on how you view yourself—your identity—and what you're capable of.

BOUNCE BACK ASSIGNMENT:

Take one or two of the following. **Own them as your own.**
Consider creating a screen saver with one of these positive
phrases emblazoned on it.

1. I'm the type of person who makes the world say "yes" to me.

2. I am an indomitable spirit. Nothing can keep me down.

3. I am a phoenix rising from the ashes.

4. A lesser person would crumble right now…but not MOI!

5. Come on, world: I dare you to take another swat. I've got
what it takes to come back swinging—and winning, dammit.

tip#

Enjoy a view with a Rumi.

BOUNCE BACK ASSIGNMENT:

Whenever you're feeling bummed, enjoy my favorite poem from this 13th-century Persian poet.

❄ ❄ ❄ ❄ ❄ ❄ ❄ ❄ ❄ ❄ ❄ ❄

GUEST HOUSE *by Rumi*

This being human is a guest house
Every morning a new arrival.
A joy, a depression, a meanness,
some momentary awareness comes
as an unexpected visitor.
Welcome and entertain them all!
Even if they are a crowd of sorrows,
who violently sweep your house
empty of its furniture,
still treat each guest honorably.
He may be clearing you out for some new delight.
The dark thought, the shame, the malice,
meet them at the door laughing,
and invite them in.
Be grateful for whoever comes,
because each has been sent
as a guide from beyond.

tip#

Perform your own research studies on happiness.

During challenging times, it's hard to believe that happiness exists. But it does. It's out there. It's up to you to find it. It could be right next door—with your neighbor. Or in the office across from you—with a colleague.

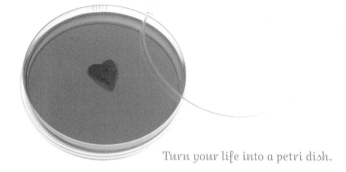

Turn your life into a petri dish.

* * * * * * * * * * * * * * *

BOUNCE BACK ASSIGNMENT:

Become your own best expert on happiness.

Make a list of people you think are happy. Now think about why. Don't stop there. Ask 25 friends, colleagues, family members, total strangers what "happiness" is— and what they do to stay as happy as possible. Then think about which techniques would work best for you.

68

When in a negatively charged state, be careful about the decisions you make.

Psychologists say there are two ways to live life: making decisions based on fear or on pleasure.

Pleasure-directed people choose to move toward what interests, enthuses, and inspires them.

Fear-directed people let fear of pain and uncertainty distract them and base decisions on avoidance.

It should be no big surprise to learn that pleasure-directed people are:

MORE happy   **LESS** controlling

MORE balanced   **LESS** jealous

MORE centered   **LESS** vindictive

 BE FOREWARNED: When you're going through an incredibly negative time, you might slip into a fear-directed state, even if it's not your natural way of being.

* * * * * * * * * * * * * * * *

Bounce Back Assignment:

Have recent events made you more **fear-directed** and thereby too focused on avoiding change, growth, awareness, uncertainty? Consciously decide to be more **pleasure-directed**—and seek out and embrace exciting new roles and pleasurable circumstances!

tip# **69**

Watch out for
repeated patterns.

Is your life like the film *Groundhog Day*? Do you keep waking up to the same problems? If you are known among friends for constantly repeating "enterpaining" stories—amusing yet disturbing tales full of doom and gloom—then you could be suffering from "emotional masochism," a universal self-sabotage syndrome.

It's like this: As children, we learn about joy from our parents.

Basically, it's as if each of us grew up feeling comfy with a certain level of happiness. Some of us are used to 90%, others only 75%, others only 17%. The point is, when this concentration shifts, even upward, a lot of us get twitchy because this new zone feels sooo unfamiliar. What do we do? We self-sabotage to shift our happiness level back down, down to what feels familiar.

The result? We experience repeated patterns of disappointment, rejection, and sorrow because this discomfort is what we've been conditioned to feel most comfortable living with.

✳ ✳ ✳ ✳ ✳ ✳ ✳ ✳ ✳ ✳ ✳ ✳ ✳ ✳ ✳ ✳

Bounce Back Assignment:

Next time you're tempted to repeat habits of self-sabotage, STOP and say the following instead: **"I am not my past behavior. I am not my past pain.** I am not how others have treated me. I am only who I think I am in this moment and what I choose to do in this moment."

tip# **70**

View change as chance.

When tough times sweep in and turn your life upside down, see change as a new chance to evolve—into a better job, a better relationship, etc. The trick? Remain clear in your ultimate goals (happiness, love, monetary security, health, fulfillment, etc.). But be flexible about who and what can bring you these things.

change

chance

* * * * * * * * * * * * *

BOUNCE BACK ASSIGNMENT:

Brainstorm **new chances** you want to pursue.

tip# **71**

Look for the

exceptions to the

rule– and let these

rule your spirit.

Just because you're going through a really rough stretch now doesn't mean you are doomed to lead a miserable life forever.

Sure, it's easy to tell yourself, "It's not my fault my life sucks! It's because this terrible, awful thing happened to me and now I'm messed up forever."

It takes real concerted effort to fight the impulse to blame your circumstances for why you're not living the life you want to be living and think you deserve. But you must put in the effort if you want to bounce back and be joyous again.

I suggest that instead of becoming a member of the Blame Culture, you sign up for membership in the We Bounced Back Impressively Culture and become one of those who really worked to overcome a major life setback.

For example, after my sexual assault, I thought about Oprah Winfrey, who was raped as a young girl, and how this event became an added impetus for her to want to become a major positive force, helping others survive difficult times. And all the countless others—Nelson Mandela, Helen Keller, Stephen Hawking, Lance Armstrong—who *transformed their greatest challenges into the greatest triumphs,* nobly and joyously inspiring others to strive for greater joy, peace, and fulfillment.

❋ ❋ ❋ ❋ ❋ ❋ ❋ ❋ ❋ ❋ ❋ ❋ ❋ ❋ ❋ ❋

Bounce Back Assignment:

You don't have to become an Oprah or Mandela to be a member of the **We Bounced Back Impressively Culture.** All you have to do is to refuse to be a victim. Your membership requires that you recognize the effort it takes to pull yourself out of the muck and mire of **blame** and **hopelessness.** Do it and **be proud.**

tip#

Follow the light blue brick road.

In life, some roads have many more lions and tigers and bears, oh my. If I'd been with Dorothy on her journey, at a certain point, I'd have suggested she consider trying a less troublesome path than her Yellow Brick Road.

Same goes for you.

If lately you feel like wicked people are forever blocking your way and houses of trouble are falling from the sky, now is the time to reassess your path.

In *The Tibetan Book of Living and Dying,* there is this wonderful poem by Portia Nelson called "Autobiography in Five Short Chapters." It describes the need to change tracks and find another path.

> **1.** I walk down the street.
> There is a deep hole in the sidewalk.
> I fall in.
> I am lost...I am hopeless.
> It isn't my fault.
> It takes forever to find a way out.

2. I walk down the same street.
There is a deep hole in the sidewalk.
I pretend I don't see it.
I fall in again.
I can't believe I am in the same place.
But it isn't my fault.
It still takes a long time to get out.

3. I walk down the same street.
There is a deep hole in the sidewalk.
I see it is there.
I still fall in…it's a habit.
My eyes are open.
I know where I am.
It is *my* fault.
I get out immediately.

4. I walk down the same street.
There's a hole in the sidewalk.
I walk around it.

5. I walk down another street.

My question to you: Are you staying on the troublesome path because it's the only path you know? Are you staying because it's the most difficult path and you think difficult is good? Are there trouble-free roads you could take? Ones that you could ease on down and still reach your goals? Are you even bothering to look for a better route, a smoother, pothole-free Brick Road?

BOUNCE BACK ASSIGNMENT:

Rebegin your journey with your ends in mind. Where do you want to be in 5 years, 10 years, 50 years? Are you on the least-bumpy, least-circuitous, least-troubled road to take you there? Remember, the best way is not always the most difficult way.

tip# **73**

Life is rarely linear.
There will always
be **zigzags** on the
way to your goals.

BOUNCE BACK ASSIGNMENT:

Keep your eyes on the prize.

As Henry Ford said, **"Obstacles are just those frightful things you see when you take your eyes off your goal."**

tip# 74

"Do not fear death
so much, but rather
the inadequate life."

—BERTOLT BRECHT

Remember, in the Introduction, I explained how bad events are as much a part of our world as gravity, and nothing will stop them from coming at us?

Well…while I was writing this book, my father became very ill, then passed away. I now use the techniques I researched for the book almost every day to help me survive this loss and stay resilient. I've also found great solace and support in one of my favorite books, Rinpoche's *Tibetan Book of Living and Dying.*

It was interesting to reread Rinpoche's book again during this challenging time. When I first read the book about a decade ago, I'd avoided reading his passages on death—thinking they didn't apply to me—as if my family and I were somehow immune to death!

Rinpoche was aware of this tendency for the healthy and vibrant to be in denial about death, and he warned us to live our lives daily knowing that death comes with a lifetime guarantee! He warns us not to become "unconscious living corpses."

Meaning? If we're not careful, we can sleepwalk through our lives— afraid to feel our deepest feelings or risk going after our truest desires.

He speaks of a Western tendency to cram our lives compulsively with unimportant activities (our to-do lists), leaving little time to do what really matters. He even jokingly renames the petty projects we call our "responsibilities" as our "irresponsiblities" because they keep us from the true tasks of living.

❋ ❋ ❋ ❋ ❋ ❋ ❋ ❋ ❋ ❋ ❋ ❋ ❋ ❋ ❋

Bounce Back Assignment:

Edit your "To-Do" list to a **"What Matters Most To Do" list** and keep it in your wallet to look at regularly. Find the time to be with loved ones, do your signature strengths, speak truthfully, give generously.

tip#

For best results,
apply regularly.

+LIFE PAIN RELIEF

I want to end this book on a happy note. And I want your life story to have a happy ending! And so I'm leaving you with one of my favorite Buddhist tales called "Steve and Dr. Immortality"!

There once was a guy named Steve who heard about a doctor in a distant kingdom who knew the secrets of immortality. Wow! Living forever sounded like a damn good thing to Steve, so he got on a plane to the Himalayas to learn all he could from Dr. Immortality. When Steve emerged from the plane, he hailed a taxi, and gave the driver the doctor's address.

"You want to see Dr. Immortality? Hahaha," the driver laughed heartily.
"What's so funny?" asked Steve.
"That quack just died about an hour ago," said the driver.
"Darn," said Steve, mightily disappointed. "If only I'd taken an earlier flight!"
"What do you mean?" asked the driver, chuckling. "If Dr. Immortality died, that means the guy didn't know the secrets to immortality at all."

Now it was Steve's turn to chuckle. "Not necessarily," he said. "Knowing how to do something and the skill of application are two entirely different things. Dr. Immortality might have very well known all the things he needed to do to live an immortal life—but he just didn't bother to do any of them!"

I agree with Steve—BIG time.

✳ ✳ ✳ ✳ ✳ ✳ ✳ ✳ ✳ ✳ ✳ ✳ ✳ ✳ ✳ ✳

Bounce Back Assignment:

It's one thing to read all the Tips in this book, it's another thing to **act on them**. Now it's up to you to **apply all these insights** and incorporate them into your daily life so you will bounce back higher, stronger, wiser!

I invite you to share with me your success stories—tell me how you transformed your tale of woe into a tale of wow and are now a better person for all you've been through.

Write to me at karen@notsalmon.com—and keep checking my site, because **I plan to give seminars** across the country on Bouncing Back. I'd love to meet you in person so we can give each other a big supportive hug because, hey, there can never be too many hugs in this world!

♡–Karen

KAREN SALMANSOHN was a Senior VP creative director at a New York ad agency who left her job to pursue her passion—writing. She is now a best-selling author (with over 1 million books sold) and the host of a Sirius radio show, "Be Happy, Dammit," inspired by the best-selling book of the same title. Other books include *Even God Is Single (So Stop Giving Me a Hard Time)* and *Quickie Stickies*. For more, visit www.notsalmon.com.